YOUR HUMAN DESIGN

Discover Your Unique Life Path & How to Navigate It with Purpose

Shayna Cornelius
and Dana Stiles

CREATORS OF DAYLUNA™

Contents

Introduction   5

9   **CHAPTER 1:**

Everything
Is Energy,
Including You

12   **CHAPTER 2:**

What Is
Human Design?

20   **CHAPTER 3:**

The Five
Types

91   **CHAPTER 4:**

The Eight
Authorities

130   **CHAPTER 5:**

Combining
Strategy and
Authority

135   **CHAPTER 6:**

Deeper Dive:
Centers

150 CHAPTER 7:

Deeper Dive:
Profiles

159 CHAPTER 8:

Deeper Dive:
Channels and
Gates

166 CHAPTER 9:

Deeper Dive:
Cross of
Incarnation

169 CHAPTER 10:

Tying It All
Together

About the Authors   172

Index   174

Introduction

THERE ARE 7.9 BILLION PEOPLE ON THE PLANET, and every single one is unique. We hear this all the time and our eyes glaze over—"Yeah, duh, no two people are the same, I get it." But then we go about our daily lives trying to operate *just* like everyone else around us. Why is that? Why do we want to be unique and also want to fit in with the status quo? Why do we measure our success in comparison to other people? Why do we feel a desire to break the mold while simultaneously trying to mold ourselves to others?

There are three major reasons that keeps us from living as our true unique selves: The first is a desire for acceptance. We want to belong somewhere, and we feel that if we allowed ourselves to be fully different and unique, then we wouldn't be accepted by those around us. We *want* to fit in because the alternative is feeling like an outsider or knowing only people who just don't understand us.

The second reason is that we don't actually know what makes us unique. Unless you are someone who popped out knowing exactly who you are and what you are here to do (which happens, but is rare), you have no clue what makes you stand apart from other people. Chances are, if you are reading this book, you are either just starting out on your spiritual journey or you have tried every spiritual modality under the sun and still feel lost. No matter where you are in life right now, the main questions you are probably asking yourself are, "Who the F am I?" "Why am I here?" and "What's my life's purpose?"

The third reason is our conditioning. We are conditioned to believe that things just are the way they are, that everyone feels the way we do, and that to truly believe you are unique is narcissistic or selfish. Beliefs such as "That's just how the world works," "Life is not meant to be easy," and "Everyone hates their job, but you have to pay the bills" are common and are at the core of our society. Although we can understand that everyone is unique, we still compare ourselves to those around us. If we see someone who is successful, we assume they worked harder than we have, they are smarter than we are, and we are not good enough. But if we are all unique, why would we all have the same path to success, love, fulfillment, and the like? The truth is, *you are meant to use your unique gifts every single day*, and that will lead you to success that only you can achieve. And here's the real kicker: It is meant to be easy.

In this book, we will talk about how you can find true acceptance for who you are and reveal the specific details of what makes *you* unique. We will talk about how to start living your purpose today and how you can release conditioning along the way—all in a way that feels easy, and most importantly, feels like you.

How to Use This Book

1 **Generate your Human Design chart** (you can do so online, including on daylunalife.com). Keep your chart nearby as you read.

2 **Look at what your chart says** next to the categories of Type, Strategy, and Authority.

3 **When you get to the Type and Authority chapters,** read the sections on the specific Type and Authority that is on your chart. Each person is only one of the five Types; thus, only one of the Types in the Type chapter will apply to you. Similarly, each person has one of the eight Authorities; thus, only one Authority in the Authority chapter will apply to you.

4 **Experiment with the strategies, tips, and daily practices** laid out for your Strategy, Authority, centers, and Profile and observe any shifts that begin to take place in your life.

THE WORLD WOULD BE A BETTER PLACE if everyone knew that they were loved. Receiving love and giving love starts within yourself. It starts with self-discovery.

When you begin to understand yourself, you begin to find authentic acceptance for yourself.

When you find acceptance for yourself, you begin to find unconditional love for yourself.

When you find love for yourself, you can give it unconditionally to others.

It's a beautiful cycle that begins with you!

CHAPTER 1

Everything Is Energy, Including You

WHEN WE THINK OF WHO WE ARE, most of us think of a mind living inside a physical human body. A brain and a body—that's all we are. We have been conditioned to see ourselves this way. With Western medicine and modern science at the forefront of our societal conditioning, we are taught to see the world through only our five physical senses. We are taught that the only things that are "real" are the things we can see, touch, taste, smell, and hear.

Of course, we know that there are real things beyond what we can sense with the naked eye. After all, we have created technologies that can detect radio waves, microwaves, and sonic waves. Within these invisible wave forms, we are able to transmit information. Even in our collective conditioned view of reality, we still can recognize that there is more going on than what we can perceive. Physical objects that appear to be solid are less than 1 percent matter and more than 99 percent energy. This means that everything in our world, including us, is mostly energy.

So why, when we look at our physical body, do we still see it as the full extent of who we are? The answer is simple: Our reality is based on our beliefs, and our beliefs are, by default, based on our conditioning. However, this reality we have all been conditioned to experience is only a small part of the truth of what we really are.

Each person has an energetic body, an electromagnetic energy field that functions in a specific way based on their design. We call this subtle energy body their aura. When you walk into a room, your aura extends past your physical body in all directions and can be felt by others. When someone is in your presence, an energetic exchange happens between your auras before you even open your mouth. Your aura communicates something about you in a powerful, nonverbal way. Although this energetic exchange is a prominent aspect of our social interactions, the majority of us don't realize it is happening because of our beliefs about reality, our lack of awareness, and our conditioning.

What Is Conditioning?

Our reality is based on our beliefs.

Our beliefs are the constructs that we create and build over time. They define our understanding of ourselves and life in general. Most of us have little awareness of what our beliefs are and no awareness that most of our beliefs about life and even ourselves are not actually our own. They are concepts that we have adopted from the world around us: what we think a "normal" life should look like, what we think are "positive qualities" in a person, how much money we "should" have, the way we "should" build a career, the way we "should" process our emotions. The list goes on. Homogenization, the pressure to be the same, has been a driving force infused into our social structure, our economy, and our educational systems. Our environment is woven by the threads of these socially agreed-upon ideals.

The problem with this is that the person we are taught we *should* be might look different from the person we actually *are*.

Psychologists have long questioned what it is that makes us who we are— nature or nurture. Through the lens of Human Design, your design is your nature and your conditioning is your nurture.

Identifying

When we identify with something, we associate that thing with a part of ourselves.

For example, many of us have been taught that being hardworking is a good quality to have. We know that if we are hardworking, people will like us, respect us, and include us in their lives. We push ourselves past our natural limits so we can be more hardworking, and eventually we feel burnt out from constantly trying to *prove* that we are hardworking. Our mind clings to this word and we pride ourselves on embodying it. It makes us feel right instead of wrong. We begin to judge other people who aren't hardworking. We get offended and feel the need to aggressively defend ourselves if someone questions our work ethic. Meanwhile, deep down, we don't actually feel good about any of this. We judge ourselves, secretly wondering whether we are lazy. We feel drained and resentful or jealous of others who seem to always be taking time off to travel or relax. This whole downward spiral happens because we identified with a quality that we were conditioned to believe is good but actually goes against our true nature.

It's a normal part of life to be influenced by the world around us, and not all conditioning impacts us negatively. However, when we are deeply identified with our conditioning, it can be hard to feel what our true nature really is.

Some people have spent decades trying to convince themselves that they *are* the qualities they have identified with. For these people, discovering their true self through Human Design is a bit shocking; it's like a magician has dramatically pulled a tablecloth away, revealing the tabletop beneath. It can feel overwhelming. But underneath, at the core, is a feeling of the instant recognition of truth.

Deconditioning

So, how do you discover what is actually you and what is your conditioning?

With your Human Design chart, you can see a clear blueprint of your true nature. All the conditioning that you may have been identifying with throughout your life simply melts away when you begin to understand, accept, and actually live as your true self. Embracing your design is not about becoming something new, but rather shedding learned behaviors to uncover who you have always been underneath. This process is called deconditioning.

CHAPTER 2

What Is Human Design?

HUMAN DESIGN IS A TOOL that can help us navigate life in personal alignment.

When we first discovered Human Design, we could not believe we had never heard of it. It provides an incredibly specific outline of how to be your authentic self, and it straight-up tells you who you are, how to make aligned decisions, and what your life purpose is. Up until recently, there hasn't been one modality that can actually point you in the direction of your unique life path . . . so what *is* Human Design and where does it come from?

Simply put, Human Design is the science of differentiation. It breaks down exactly why and how we are each different as individuals. Human Design provides a personalized handbook on how you can move through life and the world around you in a way that is energetically correct for you so that you experience less resistance, more success, harmonious connections, divine timing, and flow in your day-to-day life. Best of all, it provides you with specific instructions on how to magnify your aura and magnetically attract the life of your dreams one day at a time, in a way that feels right for you. Sound too good to be true? We thought the same thing, but after one month of experimenting with our designs, we proved to ourselves it was possible. Years later, we are still asking ourselves whether it really gets to be this easy!

Basics of Human Design

Human Design was constructed in 1987 by Ra Uru Hu. He went into an eight-day meditation in Ibiza and channeled a consciousness called The Voice, which told him about Human Design and exactly how it worked. At the same time, a massive supernova was visible to the naked eye on Earth—in Chile. It blasted the Earth with three times more neutrinos than we normally receive (more on this later), which may be why Ra's connection to The Voice was so potent.

Although Human Design was channeled in more recent times, it synthesizes four ancient modalities:

- **Western Astrology:** The Western astrology system uses the zodiac constellation placements in the sky the day and time you were born. Human Design uses astrology from the time you were born (conscious gifts) and approximately 88 days prior to your birth, when your consciousness was formed in the womb (subconscious gifts). Like astrology, Human Design uses the zodiac system, but it breaks each zodiac archetype up into smaller archetypes with the I Ching.

- **The I Ching:** A divination tool also known as The Book of Changes, the I Ching dates back to the Zhou dynasty in ancient China. Sticks (or coins) are thrown to guide the user to a meaning found in poetic writing. The book contains 64 hexagram possibilities for how the sticks land; each hexagram has a unique meaning. Human Design uses these hexagram symbols, six-lined structures in which each line is either full (yang) or broken (yin). Each of the 64 hexagrams represents a sub-archetype in the zodiac wheel that corresponds to one of the 64 gates in the bodygraph.

- **The Hindu Brahmin Chakra System:** The chakra system originated in ancient India in the Vedas. This traditional system comprises seven chakras: root, sacral, solar plexus, heart, throat, third eye, and crown. A chakra can be described as a center in the body where energy is processed. The Human Design bodygraph includes these seven chakras plus two additional energy centers: the spleen and the G center. Human Design offers the theory that *Homo sapiens* have experienced definitive points of collective evolution on an energetic level and will continue to evolve with a new shift occurring in the near future. The last evolutionary shift, which occurred in 1781, caused a change in the structure of our internal energetic workings. It resulted in a transition from our species operating with seven energy centers to operating with nine.

- **The Kabbalah Tree of Life:** The Tree of Life is a geometrical symbol from the Zohar/Kabbalistic tradition. It has been described as a map of consciousness and creation. Within the Tree of Life structure, energy flows through channels from one center to the next. This concept of energetic pathways between centers is displayed in the channels, gates, and circuitry of Human Design.

Note: You do not need to understand how each of these systems works to fully implement Human Design, but we invite you to give reverence and gratitude to each of these modalities. You can seek out other resources to learn more about them if you feel called.

All of this comes together to create a diagram of your energetic body (or aura), which Human Design calls your bodygraph. Your bodygraph allows you to see how your energy best operates in the world around you and what energetic alignment looks like for you as an individual.

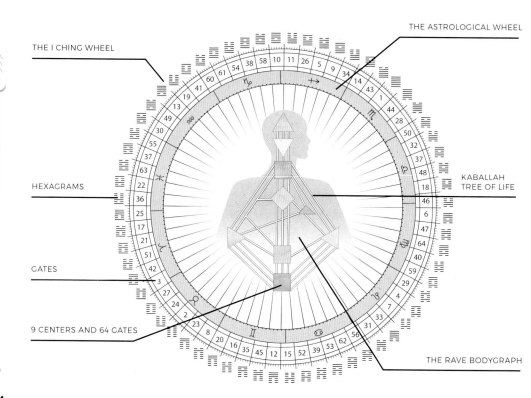

THE ASTROLOGICAL WHEEL

THE I CHING WHEEL

HEXAGRAMS

GATES

9 CENTERS AND 64 GATES

KABALLAH TREE OF LIFE

THE RAVE BODYGRAPH

The Science Behind Human Design

Human Design combines these systems with modern science, including genetics and quantum mechanics. The most important scientific foundation of Human Design is the study of neutrinos. The Voice told Ra Uru Hu that the neutrino stream, a field of subatomic particles that is created by cosmic rays, is the vehicle in which life-force energy travels through the universe. The neutrino stream is also called the breath of the stars; it is what mystics of the past called prana or chi. Neutrinos are infinitesimal cosmic messengers that carry and deliver consciousness.

From a scientific standpoint, neutrinos are considered dark matter that can pass through all matter but are extremely difficult to detect. Scientists have been baffled by neutrinos since they were discovered in 1956. The most significant thing The Voice told Ra about neutrinos is that they carry mass. This allows them to pick up and leave behind information when they pass through matter. This was huge—the discovery of neutrinos' ability to carry mass was not made in the scientific world until 1998, and Ra downloaded this information from The Voice in 1987!

This explains why your birth date, time, and location are the basis for generating your unique Human Design. When your consciousness is formed in the womb (approximately 88 days prior to your birth) and when you exit the womb at birth, the neutrino stream imprints onto your being, creating your design. Our sun and others stars emit the neutrino stream (carrying life-force energy), which passes through all the massive planets in our solar system at the current placement in their orbit, picking up information (and characteristics) from those planets and depositing tiny bits of that information into your being, programming your unique design with the flavor of the current cosmic energy. In short, you have the unique energetic traits that you do because of the qualities of the planetary energy that existed in the cosmos around the time of your birth.

The other amazing aspect of Human Design is its correlation to our genetics and DNA. Within our physical DNA, there are 64 DNA codons, and within our energetic body, there are 64 I Ching hexagrams. These 64 codons and 64 hexagrams mirror each other perfectly by both having a six-lined, binary structure. There are six groups of amino acids per codon (our genetic code) and six lines in an I Ching hexagram.

It is truly fascinating how a system that is so spiritual in practice can also mirror back the physical sciences in our collective mental awareness.

How to Locate Your Human Design Chart

To generate your Human Design chart, go to our website, daylunalife.com. You will need your exact:

- **Birth year, month, and day**

- **Birth time** (It is important to be as precise as possible, so look on your birth certificate, ask your mom, call the hospital where you were born, or book a session with an astrologer who specializes in birth time rectification. If all else fails, you can make an estimate, but please be aware that you will not generate a 100 percent accurate chart.) Make sure you are putting in 24-hour time. So, if you were born at 6:42 p.m., make sure you input 18:42. Similarly, if you were born at half past midnight, input 00:30.

- **Birth location** by country, state/province, and city

Elements of a Human Design Chart

Once you have generated your chart, you will see the following categories at the top:

- **Type:** Your Type/aura

- **Definition:** The rate at which you process new information and connect with others around you

- **Strategy:** The practice that helps you operate in alignment and create ease

- **Profile:** Your conscious and unconscious personality archetype

- **Inner Authority:** The process by which you are designed to make decisions

- **Not-Self Theme:** The feeling you'll experience when you are out of alignment

- **Incarnation Cross:** Your unique life purpose and the energy you are here to be in this world

Under that, you will then see an image of your bodygraph showing your nine centers and the lines (channels) connecting them. The centers that are white are

Type: **Projector**

Profile: **2/4**

Definition: **Triple Split Definition**

Inner Authority: **Emotional - Solar Plexus**

Strategy: **Wait for the Invitation**

Not-Self Theme: **Bitterness**

Incarnation Cross: **Right Angle Cross of Contagion (29/30 | 8/14)**

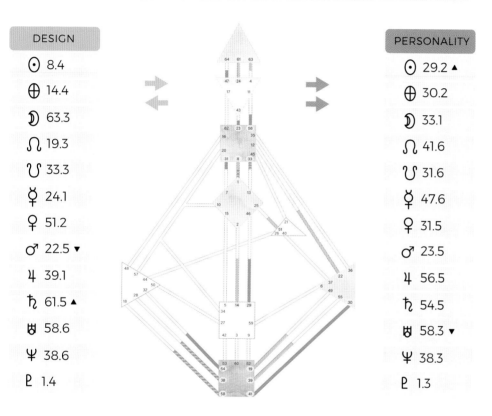

DESIGN	PERSONALITY
☉ 8.4	☉ 29.2 ▲
⊕ 14.4	⊕ 30.2
☽ 63.3	☽ 33.1
☊ 19.3	☊ 41.6
☋ 33.3	☋ 31.6
☿ 24.1	☿ 47.6
♀ 51.2	♀ 31.5
♂ 22.5 ▼	♂ 23.5
♃ 39.1	♃ 56.5
♄ 61.5 ▲	♄ 54.5
♅ 58.6	♅ 58.3 ▼
♆ 38.6	♆ 38.3
♇ 1.4	♇ 1.3

undefined, and the centers that are colored are defined; it doesn't matter what color they are.

These are just the basic elements of your Human Design chart. Throughout this book, we break down how to apply these teachings in your daily life.

17

Experimenting with Living Your Design

Your chart carries incredible depth and a vast amount of information. We will not get into every possible layer of information it contains; instead, we will focus mainly on the three most foundational and *applicable* aspects of Human Design: Type, Strategy, and Authority.

We will cover how to implement these practices, but it's up to you to experiment with practicing them in your daily life. We recommend that you choose an amount of time (two weeks to one month) and set the intention to follow your Strategy and Authority as much as you can in that time.

CHAPTER 3

The Five Types

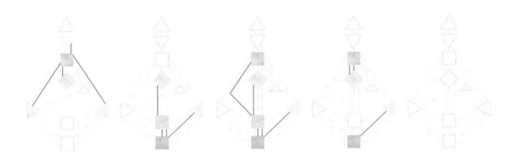

THERE ARE FIVE TYPES IN HUMAN DESIGN: Manifestor, Generator, Manifesting Generator, Projector, and Reflector. Your Type tells you how your aura exchanges energy with others and how your energy is designed to operate in general. Your Type is determined by the defined centers in your chart and the way those defined centers connect with each other. We will cover what a center is in more detail later on.

Each of the five Types has an energetic role to play and an overall contribution their energy makes to the world. Manifestors are here to impact and initiate new growth in others, Generators and Manifesting Generators are here to spread creative energy as they build what they love, Projectors are here to guide the energy use of others, and Reflectors are here to gauge the overall health and authenticity of the world around them.

Manifestors

QUICK FACTS

- **AURA:** Closed and Impactful
- **STRATEGY:** To Inform
- **SELF THEME:** Peace
- **NOT-SELF THEME:** Anger
- **HERE TO:** Initiate and Inspire

Manifestors

Manifestors comprise around 9 percent of the population.

The Manifestor aura is closed and repelling. As a Manifestor, you are designed to be extremely independent. You can find inspiration around what you want to do next completely on your own. Your closed aura protects you from outside influence, but it also blocks people from being able to read you.

Your aura is the most impactful of the five Types and can be felt strongly when you walk into a room. Because of the repelling aspect of your aura, your energy may challenge certain people, causing them to contract and draw back from you, whereas it will greatly inspire, excite, and attract others. The energetic reaction people have to your aura helps you discover who is aligned for you and who is not.

Your aura also acts as an amplifier, giving your words and actions the power to manifest your desires into reality and to ignite energy in other people. Whether you realize it or not, the small things you do and say are constantly acting as catalysts of change for others. When you speak, energy starts moving.

Although Manifestors get powerful surges of energy for taking action, they do not have a defined sacral center. This means that you are designed to have an inconsistent flow of energy that comes in cycles of highs and lows. You may be super inspired and decide to work twelve hours a day for two weeks and then take two weeks off to rest, or you may want to work Mondays, Wednesdays, and Fridays only. Whatever your energy levels are, it is important for you to be independent in deciding when, where, and how you will work.

Your energy is infused with the force needed to start new things—to initiate. However, you are not designed to have a consistent source of energy to see things through to completion. In fact, the number one way for you to burn out is to try to do things all by yourself. Your energy flows best when you get to start something new and can move on when you no longer feel called to work on that thing. Through sharing your creations and allowing a team to help finish what you've started, you offer the team something new and different to work on and you free yourself up for your next exciting venture.

As a Manifestor, you are here to do what you want, when you want, because you want to! This sounds too good to be true, but when you allow yourself the freedom you desire, you start to see your world open up in unimaginable ways. Because freedom is such a big theme in your life, you can easily find yourself falling into one of two categories: people-pleasing or super rebellious.

You can easily find yourself falling into one of two categories: people-pleasing or super rebellious.

Both sides of this spectrum come from a fear of being controlled. Because your energy is so impactful to others, the people in your life want to know what you are thinking, feeling, and planning on doing next. But because your aura is closed, they can't get a sense of what you're going to do the way they can for other people. This can leave them wary or even fearful of your plans, causing them to try to control you to create a sense of predictability. You can find yourself walking on eggshells to avoid pushback from others. You do not want to be disruptive or be told what to do, so you decide to just please others and not be too bold. Bold = seen = critiqued = controlled. Conversely, when people try to control you, you can respond through rebellion. You can say F you to the world and go even further out of your way to do the exact opposite of what someone wants you to do. This is all because Manifestors are not here to be told what to do! You simply do not need advice, validation, or any kind of external stimuli the way other people do.

It is normal to teeter-totter between people-pleasing and rebellion throughout your life; however, the sweet spot is right in the middle. When you can say, "I'm doing this because I want to and I love and respect you," that is alignment for you. Yes, you can do what you want. And yes, you can be polite and considerate while doing it.

So how do you initiate, share your ideas, have freedom, and allow others to complete things with and for you? By leaning into your Strategy!

STRATEGY: TO INFORM

Your Strategy in Human Design is how you are designed to operate on a daily, moment-to-moment basis. If you think of your energetic body like a car, your Strategy is telling you *how* to drive your car. What is the best way for you to navigate the road and the other cars around you?

As a Manifestor, your Strategy in life is to inform. Yes, this means speaking out loud. It means informing the people and world around you of everything you are thinking, feeling, dreaming up, and wanting to do—before you do it!

We know, this does not sound enticing to you. That is because Manifestors are the only Type whose Strategy does not come naturally to them. You just want to be left alone to do your own thing and it shouldn't matter to other people what you are doing, right? Well, because your aura is closed, the only way to decrease the amount of resistance and increase the amount of support you get from the people in your life is by letting them into your world through informing. When you open up a line of communication, you open up a window into your closed aura, letting people peer inside to understand what you want and need.

Other people can't read your mind, and neither can the universe. To manifest your dreams, you literally have to say them out loud. The universe wants to give you everything you desire, but because of your closed aura, it doesn't know what you want unless you say it. Informing is the most important thing you will ever do. In fact, if you were to decide to inform everyone and the universe of every single thought that popped into your head for two weeks, your life would radically change. However, informing is not all-or-nothing; it's more like a sliding scale. The more you do it, the more you will see your life improve. The less you do it, the slower it might take for your dreams to actualize.

Here is how to get started with informing:

- **What to inform:** Any decision, feeling, dream, struggle, desire, or thought that pops into your head

- **When to inform:** After you've decided to do something but before you act on it

- **Whom to inform:** The universe and all the people in your life who could be impacted by what you're doing or feeling

There is nothing too small to inform about. Informing can be as simple as saying, "I'm going to the store; I'll be back in ten minutes," "I've changed my mind about taking on this project," "I don't feel like talking right now," or "I just need a little alone time, so I'm going to eat dinner in my room tonight." You will be shocked at how people respond with support and understanding. Any time you experience resistance from others, it is usually because you informed too late or not at all. For example, if you just went into your room and closed the door, you may come out to find your partner is hurt and annoyed with you. Whereas, if you inform first (no matter how trivial it may seem to you), your partner will gladly give you your space, no questions asked, because they understand your needs.

The more you let people in by speaking *before* doing, the more you will see the world rallying to support you with anything you need.

MAGNETIZING YOUR AURA BY HONORING YOUR URGES

As a Manifestor, you can channel new ideas and innovations to share with the world. You get these new ideas on a daily basis through urges. Urges are significant experiences and are unique to Manifestors. An urge is a powerful, sudden desire or inspiration to take action or create something. The urges you get are here to guide you toward divine timing and catalyze others. Urges are not meant to be rationalized. If you can't explain a sudden desire to do something, that is a good way to know it is an urge!

We invite you to think of your urges as sparks. When you receive a spark, it's your job to release it into the world by saying it out loud. Some of the sparks you release might catch fire in your own life. Others might catch fire in someone else's life, and others might fizzle out, never catching fire at all. It is not your job to worry about whether your sparks will catch fire; it's your job to honor the sparks that come to you by voicing them. If a spark that you vocalize sticks with you for some time and keeps calling you, it may be catching fire in your own life. This is when you can use your Authority to decide whether you want to feed and grow that fire (e.g., start a business, start a project, hire employees). Once a fire has grown in your life, it can be tempting to spend all your time tending to that fire. You must remember that you are not the fire or the fire tender; you are the creator of sparks.

> ## You are not the fire or the fire tender; you are the creator of sparks.

A lot of Manifestors stop themselves from sparking fires in the world because they fear sharing something before it is fully conceptualized, believing it may be criticized or plagiarized. However, that spark might be meant for someone else and you are meant to initiate them with it. We like this spark analogy because it helps Manifestors see that while they can be powerful creators, the pressure is off for them to force or maintain their creations. The most important role they play is in having the potential to be

DAILY PRACTICE

1 **Select an amount of time between two weeks and one month.** During this time, begin informing as much as possible.

2 **Pay attention to your urges.** Your most aligned action comes from listening to these internal desires/impulses.

3 **Create space for rest and alone time.** Your body will guide you towards when you need these things.

4 **Any time you hit resistance, burnout, fatigue, or misunderstanding,** inform even more. This will always smooth things out and get everything back on track.

a fire starter without attachment to the outcome. It's not your responsibility to judge your urges. It's your responsibility to pay attention to them and voice them, releasing new potential into the world.

SELF THEME AND NOT-SELF THEME

It might be strange to hear that you are designed to be a super impactful, inspiring self-starter. That is because your self theme, the feeling you'll get when you are in alignment, is peace. You are happiest when you get to chill, when you feel free to be who you are, and when you are left alone to do your own thing and everyone else honors and respects that. The beautiful part about being a Manifestor is that when you create peace in your life through informing, you align with the power of your design and are able to effortlessly impact and inspire others with every breath.

Feeling peaceful is the goal, but it's easy to neglect to inform, which closes people out of your life and creates resistance from others. Receiving too much resistance can cause you to slip out of alignment and experience your not-self theme of anger. Anger can feel like spurts of white-hot rage, an upsetting feeling of disturbance, or a strong annoyance at the people and the world around you.

CONDITIONING FOR MANIFESTORS

Some of the main conditioning you face as a Manifestor is the expectation that you should dim your light to fit in. With your powerful aura, you may have been told that you are "too much" or too intense. There can be a tendency to shy away from being seen or to lie about who you are and what you feel to ensure you are accepted. You may feel that if you are your boldest self, you cause unwanted drama. Because all you really want is peace, hiding can be extremely tempting. You can conclude that no one will ever understand you and that you are destined to be alone. However, this cannot be further from the truth! Manifestors are extremely alluring and magnetic when they embrace their impactfulness. The people who are right for you are drawn to what you have to say and would love to help support you and your visions.

Your other biggest conditioning is around the way you work. You can feel pressure to have consistent energy levels and always finish what you start. When you find it difficult to embody these qualities, you may judge yourself and push yourself to work even harder. This conditioning can make it hard to let go of the need to prove you can do it all, and it can make it hard to trust other people to contribute, especially on projects you've initiated. You may even fear that no one else will be able to do something the way you want it to be done. The more you control and micromanage, the more you keep yourself playing small. When you allow other people to take what you've started and run with it, you will start seeing your creations reach higher levels of success.

Other conditioned beliefs can include:

- Your desires make you selfish.
- You are not a leader.
- You are not special, so you should play small.
- It's your job to make sure people feel comfortable all the time.
- You are always being judged.
- You have to have all the answers before moving forward.
- No one will love you if they know who you really are.

Work

Freedom and flexibility are vital for Manifestors to have a healthy work environment; they need to be able to work on what they want, when they want to. Often Manifestors find themselves working for themselves; however, they can work for others if they have a healthy work/life balance with enough freedom to choose their projects and how they spend their time. Manifestors have bursts of energy, which can look like anything from working five hours a day on one project to working two weeks straight and then taking two weeks off completely for a different project. Having a rigid, consistent 9-to-5 job will feel draining over time, even if they love what they do.

Physical Body and Sleep

When it comes to diet and exercise, it is best for Manifestors to eat what they want and work out in the way they want to. If they try to conform to what others are doing, they will not be able to digest their food properly and the physical exercise they partake in will drain them. When going to bed, Manifestors should go to bed before they are tired and take an hour to clear out and wind down and allow their energy to settle before trying to fall asleep.

Children

Manifestor children know how to parent themselves from a young age. As a parent, it is best to let the Manifestor child take the lead in how they want to spend their energy each day. To help them embody their Strategy of informing, the parent can simply model proper informing often. Leading by example (instead of telling what to do) will naturally encourage the Manifestor child to reciprocate informing.

Relationships

It's important that Manifestors initiate romantic partners into a relationship. Making the first move can be taboo in our conditioning (especially for Manifestor women), but that actually starts the relationship off with a healthy energetic exchange. Once a Manifestor is in a committed relationship, cultivating radically honest, vulnerable, and polite communication is paramount in relieving any tension. Partners can support their Manifestor through reciprocal informing with their daily schedule and encourage the Manifestor to take alone time when desired.

Manifestor Not-Self Theme Quiz

Select the answer that best describes your current feelings. **Keep track of how many As, Bs, and Cs you select.**

My relationship to my family and other close supportive relationships:

A   I prefer to keep my plans to myself because often the people closest to me do not respect what I want to do with my life. I would rather keep to myself than have to deal with others trying to control me or giving me resistance when I'm just trying to do my own thing.

B   I find that the people closest to me respect my freedom in some areas of life but not others. In areas where they respect my freedom, I find it easier to speak openly about how I really feel, what I want or don't want, and so on. However, in areas where they do not easily understand or accept me, I find it hard to be open and share what I'm up to.

C   I am really open and honest with others. I often share what I'm thinking, feeling, and wanting to do next, even if I don't always have it figured out. In general, the people closest to me get me and are supportive of what I want to do.

My relationship to my career/life purpose:

A   I feel stifled and limited in my current job. It bothers me to be micromanaged when I know I have the potential to lead.

B   What I'm doing now works for me because I have wiggle room in my schedule, but I crave more creative freedom to work on the things that I feel truly called to.

C   I have a lot of freedom and control around what I want to create and when I want to work. I trust that I don't need to do everything all on my own and that there can be support available to me from people who want to help me see things through to completion.

My relationship to my energy levels and physical well-being:

A   I often feel exhausted, burnt out, and over it internally, but I try to keep going and push myself to be consistent in how I show up in the world.

29

B I am beginning to embrace that my energy works in spurts of productivity and rest. Even though the world is not necessarily designed for us all to work in cycles, I trust that this is the best way for me and I'm beginning to feel how much more energized and peaceful I already feel.

C I completely trust in my cycles of productivity and rest. I have observed that when I allow myself to rest and retreat when it feels natural, I show up with much more clarity, focus, and energy when the timing is right.

My relationship to my romantic partner(s):

A I often feel like my desires and needs are not getting met. I keep waiting for my partner to step up and start treating me the way I deserve to be treated, but I haven't seen them initiating very much change.

B I am pretty open to telling my partner how I really feel and what I need to feel supported. I sometimes notice I'm waiting for them to take the lead and forget how much easier things work when I initiate growth.

C I feel completely open to sharing what I need and how I really feel as soon as it comes up. I feel free to be my full self and notice how much my partner rises to the occasion when I share something new.

My relationship with myself:

A I feel like I have to hide who I really am or what I'm really thinking because if I let myself be seen for who I really am, no one will accept me.

B I've embraced who I am and love my impactful aura. I still don't always feel comfortable sharing myself and my voice with the world, but I love the direction I'm headed in.

C I completely embrace the full me. I embrace that I am here to do what I want, when I want, and to be who I am unapologetically. I love that when I own that, it helps me be more impactful and inspiring to the world around me. I embrace that informing just helps everything feel easier in that process.

MOSTLY AS: LIVING IN YOUR NOT-SELF

If you answered mostly As, you may be living in your not-self more often than not. You may be feeling angry or resentful about the lack of freedom and authentic acceptance you have in your life, or you may be annoyed at how you are not able to fully spread your wings.

Remember that the more you inform, open up, and let people in on how you're feeling, what you want more of and less of in your life, and what your dreams are (even if those dreams are not fully fleshed out), the easier things will start to feel. You have a powerful and rare aura that operates differently from the majority of others'. Cut yourself some major slack and remember that when you accept and love your full self exactly as you are, you will naturally feel more moments of peace.

MOSTLY BS: GROWING IN THE RIGHT DIRECTION

If you answered mostly Bs, you are finding your flow around living in personal alignment. There may be moments where you still feel a bit of anger, annoyance, or pushback from others, and that's okay! It's all about having awareness of your not-self and letting it prompt you to inform, open up, and share authentically.

You are beginning to prove to yourself that the more you choose to accept yourself and free yourself from all limitations, the more you get to experience the peace and impactfulness you are here to experience.

MOSTLY CS: PEACEFUL WARRIOR

If you answered mostly Cs, you are mostly living in personal alignment! Informing will always be a conscious daily practice, but you are embodying the peaceful, self-assured, brave, open, chill yet badass Manifestor vibes the world needs from you. Remember that even when you are aligned and life feels peaceful, you still may not always see how powerfully you impact others and how your words and actions act as a catalyst for them. We invite you to celebrate yourself, celebrate your authenticity, and celebrate the fact that you are designed to have peace and impact.

TIPS AND RECOMMENDATIONS FOR LIVING YOUR DESIGN

Tips

- **SAY ALOUD THREE INTENTIONS** you have for the day every morning.
- **SAY ALOUD THREE THINGS** you are grateful for every night.
- **WHEN DECIDING TO MAKE A BIG CHANGE,** write a list of all the people this change could potentially impact. Reach out to inform those people before you take action.

Supportive Crystals

- **RED JASPER** for being bold and seen
- **PYRITE** for abundance and stating what you want with clarity
- **TIGER'S EYE** for confidence
- **ROSE QUARTZ** for compassion
- **AQUAMARINE** to help words flow with ease
- **AMAZONITE** for unifying your heart to your voice

Essential Oils

- **GERANIUM**
- **SANDALWOOD**
- **PEPPERMINT**
- **CHAMOMILE**
- **LAVENDER**

Meditations

- **IF YOU ARE DECONDITIONING FROM PEOPLE-PLEASING**, sit in meditation and envision your most fearless, fierce, badass, queen/king, highest self. Feel their vibration. Bring that frequency into your body and allow your cells to vibrate at that level.

- **IF YOU ARE DECONDITIONING FROM UNHEALTHY REBELLION**, sit in meditation and tune in to your heart space. Think of the people or pets you have the deepest, most genuine love for. Let that love grow in your heart and visualize it beaming out of you like ripples expanding in water. As you extend this love, extend a heartfelt wish for their life.

- **LIGHT A CANDLE OR BURN INCENSE, SAGE, OR PALO SANTO** and have a conversation with the universe. Start with describing how you feel or asking for any assistance you desire. See what else wants to pour out of you.

DECONDITIONING JOURNAL PROMPTS

- **On a scale of 1 to 10,** with 1 being people-pleasing and 10 being rebellious, where do I currently fall?

- **Where in my life am I afraid to be seen?**

- **In what areas of my life am I holding back?**

- **Are there people in my life** who don't understand me or with whom I often feel friction? If so, who are they and how can I start informing more with them?

- **What was my last urge or spark?** Did I say it out loud without judging or controlling it?

- **What are some small ways I can start** informing others or the universe more?

- **In what areas of my life** am I not being honest with myself and/or others?

- **List 10 things you love about yourself.** Now say them out loud.

- **List 10 things you love about the people in your life.** Now say them out loud.

Generators

QUICK FACTS

- **AURA:** Open and Enveloping
- **STRATEGY:** To Respond
- **SELF THEME:** Satisfaction
- **NOT-SELF THEME:** Frustration
- **HERE TO:** Use Their Energy Doing What They Love

Generators

Generators are among the most common of the types, comprising around 37 percent of the population.

The Generator aura is open and enveloping. As a Generator, you are designed to be receptive to everything you come across, openly taking in your environment and then discerning what you want to commit your capable, creative energy to.

All Generators have their sacral center defined. This gives you access to a consistent source of powerful life-force energy that can fuel you and energize the people around you. You are designed to use up the entirety of your energy in a satisfying way each day and then wake up the next day feeling fully recharged. There are a lot of benefits to having this sacral energy, with the most obvious being that you are able to build and finish the projects or tasks you decide to take on. When you find something you love, you can work on it for hours, completely losing track of time.

With your open and enveloping aura, your presence comes across as welcoming, nurturing, and warm. This allows you to connect easily and helps you sense what others need to feel supported. The challenge is that because people can feel that you are open, they feel like they can ask you to do things for them. With your tendency to nurture, saying yes can feel like second nature, even when it is something that you don't actually want to do. This can lead to a habit of sacrificing yourself for others, which can diminish your energy reserves, leaving you feeling completely burnt out. The remedy for this is following your Strategy.

STRATEGY: TO RESPOND

As a Generator, your Strategy is to respond. You are here to use your energy doing what you want to do, and how you discover what you want to do is through responding. The simplest definition of responding is to "act or behave in reaction to something or someone" (according to Oxford Languages). Although this definition works, Generators are not here to respond to life with their minds. Instead, they are here to respond to life with their sacral responses.

A sacral response comes from your sacral center. It is a primal gut response that arises in your lower belly and energizes your body. When you come across something that elicits a positive sacral response, it feels like an ignited energy of desire and excitement in your body that may even be instinctually vocalized as an "ooo" or an "uh-huh, yes!" A positive sacral response is your body's way of telling you that you've come across something you desire and that now is the correct time for you to engage with this thing.

If your sacral center responds to something with a decrease of energy, which may even vocalize as an "uh-uh, no," your body is telling you that you do not desire that thing at the moment and it's not in alignment for you to engage with it right now. This may change in a couple of hours, days, or weeks, but for now, you are not meant to do the thing.

Now, we want to talk about the in between stuff. What if you don't feel anything toward the thing in front of you? That is also your body telling you "no for now." This is the most common thing you might feel, and it is the hardest to say no to. You can easily end up saying yes to mediocre things because they don't result in a strong no, so you can think of reasons why they could be a yes. This is especially true if someone asks something of you (your help with a project, going to lunch, etc.), because you can feel bad and talk yourself into it.

It is so important to say "no for now" to mediocre things. They are actually where you leak your energy the most, and they can cause major burnout in your life. If you are in love with your work or career but feel exhausted all the time, checking in with your body in this way and truly saying "no for now" when you feel nothing can be a major game changer!

Here is what following these sacral responses might look like in real life: Imagine that you're looking at your morning coffee. In the core of your body, do you feel expansive, light, and easy, like you have energy to pour into making this cup of coffee? Or do you feel contraction in your gut, a pit in your stomach, or even the tiniest bit of exhaustion toward it? The expansion and energy are a "yes, now is the time for this coffee in front of me." The contraction and exhaustion are a "no, now is not the time for this coffee in front of me." If it's a no, can you go to the fridge and check in with your body there? Do you have energy to pour into making anything in there? If not, can you step outside and feel whether you have energy to go to a coffee shop? If yes, great! Now is the time to listen to what your body has told you. After following your body's call to engage, you find yourself in the coffee shop, where you overhear a conversation that inspires you to start a new business, project, or idea—or is simply exactly what you needed to hear! You would have missed it if you were at home making your coffee because it's what you "should" do.

The more you can listen to your body in this way, the better. Check in with that contraction or expansion as much as you can and honor it. Of course, there are going to be times when you feel the contraction/exhaustion and you still have to do the thing (otherwise none of us would ever do laundry again), but just noting that you are doing something that your body is not into will still increase your magnetism.

To practice the Strategy of responding in daily life, we like to break it down into asking yourself these three questions:

- "What is directly in front of me right now?"
- "How does my body feel about it?"
- "Can I listen?"

These three questions help you be fully present with the stimuli in your environment. They also help you quiet your mind's interference so you can listen to your body's internal guidance system. Because you are a Generator, your body is designed to guide you to be in the right place at the right time. As much as our minds might try, they are not connected to divine timing. It is our bodies that are connected to this divine flow.

MAGNETIZING YOUR AURA BY MANAGING YOUR FOREST

You are a magnet. As a Generator, your main priority is to magnetize your aura so life can bring you the things you desire. You do this mainly by using your Strategy and by creating space in your day-to-day life. If you are busy all the time and have no open space, there is no room in your energy for something new to be brought to you. When we want change, transition, or just for our dreams to manifest into reality, we need room for something new to come in. We cannot be at capacity.

You are a magnet.

Think of your daily energy usage as a forest full of trees. Each tree represents something you spend your time and energy doing. Some trees are healthy and thriving, while others are lifeless and dying but are still standing there taking up space. When we want change or something new, the first thing we do is plant new seeds everywhere. However, if there is no room for those seeds to take root, they cannot grow. To make space for something new, we must first manage our forest. We do this by assessing the forest, identifying the dead trees, and removing at least one of them to make some open space.

In real life, the process of managing your energetic forest looks like writing a list of all the things you did yesterday. Ask yourself: How many of them felt good and easy to do? How many of them drained you? How many of them did you *have* to do but didn't *want* to? How many of them felt just okay? From there, it's not about removing all the things that drained you, but instead removing just one to create some open space in your day tomorrow. Now, it's crucial that you don't fill that time before it comes. If you now have fifteen minutes or an hour free tomorrow, it is tempting for your mind to say, "I have free time tomorrow. What should I do?! Should I get a massage? Should I take a nap? Should I work out?" Should, should, should. It is important to resist filling that time with anything before it arrives. Instead, use your Strategy to decide how you want to spend that time in the moment when it arrives. Move your body in front of different options (e.g., your bookshelf, fridge, bed, car) and feel in your body what is being ignited. Dedicating this time to listening to your body is the best way to actively increase your magnetism.

SELF THEME AND NOT-SELF THEME

The self theme for Generators is satisfaction. When you are in alignment, you are designed to feel completely satisfied with your life in the present moment. This feeling of satisfaction is a signpost that you have used up all of your energy for the day in a way that met your desires. You are left with a warm, full-bodied feeling of contentment and fulfillment. Although this is the goal, we live in a world that teaches us that we must spend our energy doing things that we don't want to do. Neglecting your desires in small or big ways can cause you to experience your not-self theme of frustration. Frustration can feel like intense difficulty and annoyance, or it can feel like a subtle undertone of just being over something and feeling stuck.

DAILY PRACTICE

1 **Select an amount of time between two weeks and one month.** Use it to practice asking yourself what is in front of you and how your body feels about it. Can you listen? If not, just take note.

2 **Make a list of all the tasks you do in a day.** Do them while listening to your body and find one you can remove to create open space.

3 **Any time you have open space, wait for that time to arrive** and then check in with your body and whatever is directly in front of you. Move your body around until something in front of you feels expansive and is a yes from your body. Spend that time doing that thing.

4 **Have others ask you yes-or-no questions.** This makes it easier for you to hear your truth.

5 **Engage in sensual activities.** Smell your food or essential oils, turn on music and dance, feel the breeze on your face, walk barefoot on the earth, and do things that make you feel sexy and free.

CONDITIONING FOR GENERATORS

The biggest conditioning Generators face is the expectation that they put their head down and work hard on whatever is asked of them. Because Generators have the sacral energy to get things done, their energy can be taken advantage of. There is a misconception that they are here to be the worker bees of the planet, that they must work their life away in an unfulfilling 9-to-5 position in order to provide for their loved ones. This cannot be further from the truth. Generators are here to work on what they love. Doing so is their soul's mission and their biggest contribution to society. Only when they are doing what they love do they continue to generate a sustainable flow of the sacred life-force energy that nourishes the world around them.

Another powerful piece of conditioning Generators face is the belief that they must force things to happen by creating a sensible plan and sticking to it. They can feel that if they don't take the initiative to figure out what lies ahead, then nothing good will happen in their life. With this conditioning, they can struggle with a tendency to worry about their future, when they are actually designed to live in the present and be receptive to what life brings them.

Other conditioned beliefs can include:

- Your desires make you selfish.
- Things that are exciting or fun are not practical, and you cannot make money doing them.
- You are not special, so you should play small.
- You are not a leader; you are a follower.
- It's your job to make sure people feel comfortable all the time.

GENERATORS IN LIFE

Work

Generators are designed to be lit up by their work! It is vital that they work on something that they love and is satisfying for them to get into the details of. They can find that they love working as part of a team in someone else's company, or that they are the most lit up when creating their own projects or business. Either way, the most important thing is that they are truly into what they're doing and are excited to master their craft. If they're not, their work will not be sustainable or fulfilling and will cause deep frustration in all aspects of their life.

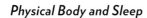

Physical Body and Sleep

It is best for Generators to listen to what they want to eat or crave in the present moment. We are conditioned to believe that if we listen to our desires all the time with food, then we will just eat junk food all day. However, when Generators truly tune in to what their body wants (and not just what their mind thinks they should want as a treat), their body will always guide them toward the nourishment they need in the moment.

Generators need to use up all of their energy each day; otherwise, they can feel restless or even anxious or depressed. They do not need time to unwind at night. Instead, it is best for them to go straight to sleep once they are tired.

Children

To help Generator children voice their sacral responses, encourage them to have big reactions and voice your own reactions to lead by example. Presenting options to them one or two at a time allows the Generator child to clearly hear what they want to do or eat. Finding tools or participating with them in activities that offer connection to the physical body (e.g., essential oils, arts and crafts, or dance) can be a fun bonding experience and help the child hone their ability to access their truth.

Relationships

The most important thing for Generators in relationships is that they have an energized and embodied sense of desire for their partner when entering into the relationship. It can be tempting to enter into a relationship because it makes sense on paper—for example, the potential partner has a good job, the correct location, and "checks all the boxes" mentally. But if there is not a true desire or pure want for that partner, then it is not a correct relationship for them. Once in a committed relationship, a supportive partner will help the Generator honor their truth/boundaries in saying "no" more and will be filled with satisfaction and joy when they are together.

Generator Not-Self Theme Quiz

Select the answer that best describes your current feelings. **Keep track of how many As, Bs, and Cs you select.**

My relationship to my family and other close supportive relationships:

A   I often find myself taking care of everyone in my family even when I don't want to. I feel pressure to help out and feel guilty if I don't show up at gatherings even though while I'm there, I usually wish I was somewhere else.

B   I'm getting better at saying no when I'm not actually lit up by helping, although I'm not perfect at it. At first it was hard to feel like I was letting people down, but now I'm finding that when I honor what my body wants more often, I have more energy, space, and clarity about the ways I do want to help my loved ones.

C   I only help out or give when I genuinely want to for the most part. As I follow my own joy more and more, I've been noticing how much positive energy I've been spreading to my family.

My relationship to my career/life purpose:

A   I definitely don't feel lit up or energized by what I'm currently doing, but I also have no idea what I would want to be doing instead. I feel stuck where I currently am, but I get anxious and overwhelmed when I even think about making a change.

B   I am lit up about certain parts of what I am currently doing. However, I don't feel completely into what I am currently doing.

C   I can honestly say that I love what I do. It feels good to get to show up and pour my creativity into building, playing, and working in this realm. I feel present and energized when I am engaged with my work.

My relationship to my energy levels and physical well-being:

A   I often feel dull, stuck, and a bit stagnant with my energy to work on things. I can have trouble falling asleep or feel a lack of energy in the morning.

B I'm finding that through doing less of what I'm not into and more of what I am lit up by, I feel more energized overall.

C I feel guided by my sacral responses about how to nourish my body in every moment. By the end of the day, I've used up all of my energy and I fall into bed feeling clear and fulfilled. Each morning I wake up with a fresh tank of energy, ready to work.

My relationship to my romantic partner(s):

A I often feel like I over-give to my partner, and I don't feel like I am receiving what I want or need out of my relationship.

B I am starting to honor myself and my needs more. I notice that the more connected I am to my sensuality and what brings me joy, the deeper and more nourishing my relationships feel.

C My romantic partnership is full of depth, warmth, joy, and healthy boundaries. I feel encouraged to follow my joy and also feel supported in saying no when I want to. My relationship helps me to be even more in tune with my body.

My relationship with myself:

A I don't really know what's special about myself, what I'm into, or where I belong. I'm feeling a bit lost at the moment.

B I feel like I've really begun finding who I am through paying attention to the things my sacral center responds to. I sometimes get hung up on questioning myself or my future, but overall I am discovering where I want to go and how I'm meant to use my gifts in this world through discovering what lights me up.

C I fully appreciate the fact that I am a creative being and that I am here to build whatever I want to in this lifetime. I see how easily I connect with people and bring people together, and I love that all I have to do to use my energy correctly is follow my sacral responses.

MOSTLY AS: LIVING IN YOUR NOT-SELF

If you answered mostly As, you may be living in your not-self more often than not. You may be feeling frustrated or stuck quite frequently because you have been using your energy doing what others think you should do instead of what you actually want to do.

The more you focus on being present and listening to what your body responds to with energy and excitement, the more you will be guided toward where to correctly spend your energy. This will lead you back to your natural aligned state of satisfaction. Following your sacral responses may sound simple, but it is no easy feat with the way we are conditioned to work and show up for other people. Be gentle on yourself, and when you catch yourself feeling frustrated, remember that you always have the power to tune in to your inner compass with your sacral responses.

MOSTLY BS: GROWING IN THE RIGHT DIRECTION

If you answered mostly Bs, you are finding your flow around living in personal alignment. There may be moments where you still feel frustrated, and that's okay! It's all about having awareness of your not-self and letting it prompt you to come back to being present, managing your forest, and responding.

You are beginning to prove to yourself that the more you follow what lights you up, the more you magnetically attract the right opportunities, inspirations, and connections that bring you so much satisfaction.

MOSTLY CS: SATISFIED CREATIVE BEING

If you answered mostly Cs, you are mostly living in personal alignment! You are experiencing life as a flowing, fulfilled, lit-up Generator who exudes the powerful life-force energy that the world needs from you.

Remember that even when you are aligned and you feel satisfied with how you are spending your energy each day, your inner guidance only really operates in the present. We invite you to lean in to trusting your body's wisdom, trusting that you are a magnetic being, and trusting that the inspiration and opportunities around what's next will find you.

TIPS AND RECOMMENDATIONS FOR LIVING YOUR DESIGN

Tips

- SING IN THE CAR OR SHOWER to open up your throat chakra to free your sacral sounds.
- CONSIDER ONE OPTION AT A TIME when making small daily choices.
- CHECK IN WITH YOUR BODY on all the small autopilot things you do—preparing meals, doing chores, running errands, selecting clothes, and the like. These tasks are a great place to hone your ability listen to your sacral responses.
- SAY THE MANTRA, "I trust my body to guide me."

Supportive Crystals

- ORANGE CALCITE for creative energy
- TURQUOISE for joyous connection
- CITRINE for increasing confidence and magnetism
- BLACK TOURMALINE for protection from conditioning
- MORGANITE for shedding guilt
- DESERT JASPER for connection to pleasure

Essential Oils

- CINNAMON
- ORANGE BLOSSOM
- VETIVER
- YLANG-YLANG

Meditations

- **LET YOUR BODY GUIDE YOU** to an essential oil it wants to receive. Breathe in the aroma and describe the energetic shifts you feel in your body.
- **DO AN EMBODIMENT MEDITATION** by playing music that captures your current mood and dancing, stretching, or moving your body in a way that feels good.
- **TURN A MUNDANE TASK INTO A PRESENCE RITUAL** by focusing on deeply observing every physical sensation you have while doing the task.
- **TAKE A WALK IN NATURE WITHOUT A PRESCRIBED PLAN.** Tune in to your sacral responses to guide you on which direction to take, which plants to stop and check out, and how long to walk.

DECONDITIONING JOURNAL PROMPTS

- **Do I have trouble saying no to people?**
- **Do I feel that my needs or desires are selfish** or unimportant? If so, why is that?
- **How can I allow others to help me more?**
- **Do I have activities or hobbies that I love** and that feel playful for me? How often do I allow myself time to do them?
- **How can I prioritize more play in my life?**
- **What is something I am currently doing every day** (in work or in my personal life) that I can cut out to make space in my day?
- **In what areas of my life am I not being honest** with myself and/or others?
- **In what areas of my life do I find it hard to be present?** When am I most easily worried about the future?

Manifesting Generators

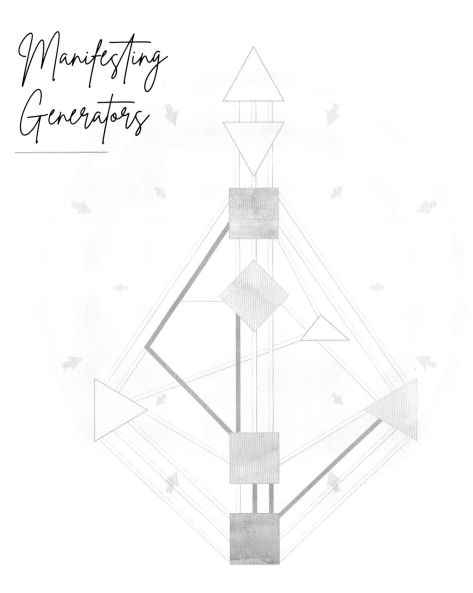

QUICK FACTS

- **AURA:** Open, Enveloping, and Impactful
- **STRATEGY:** To Respond
- **SELF THEME:** Satisfaction

- **NOT-SELF THEME:** Frustration
- **HERE TO:** Inspire and Use Their Energy In Diverse Ways Doing What They Love

Manifesting Generators

Manifesting Generators (Man-Gens or MGs for short) are among the more common of the types, as they make up around 33 percent of the population. As a Manifesting Generator, you are unique in that you are like a hybrid of two Types: Manifestor and Generator. (For this reason, we recommend you also read the Manifestor and Generator sections of this chapter.)

Manifesting Generators are technically a variation of the Generator Type. So like Generators, they have an aura that is open and enveloping. Your energetic field is receptive to all the stimuli in your environment, and you can easily connect to other people around you, just like a Generator. However, because you also have Manifestor aspects, there is a unique flavor to your aura that feels impactful, inspiring, and a bit unpredictable.

All Manifesting Generators have their sacral center defined. This gives you access to a consistent source of powerful life-force energy that can fuel you and energize the people around you. You are designed to use up the entirety of your energy in a satisfying way each day and then wake up the next day feeling fully recharged.

There are a lot of benefits to having this sacral energy, with the most obvious being that you are able to build and finish the projects or tasks you decide to take on. When you find something you love, you have the energy to work on it for hours and see it through to completion. With your open and impactful aura, your presence comes across as exciting, welcoming, and warm. This aura allows you to connect easily and helps you sense what others need to feel supported. The challenge is that because people can feel you are so open, they feel as though they can ask you to do things for them. With your tendency to connect with others, saying yes can feel like second nature, even when it is something that you don't actually want to do. This can lead to a habit of constantly sacrificing yourself for others, which can diminish your energy reserves, leaving you feeling completely burnt out.

The benefits of having this consistent sacral energy are the same as they are for a Generator. What makes a Manifesting Generator different is that you are designed to crave variety and have many different interests. Generators like to be thorough and dedicate their energy in a more singular way, whereas Man-Gens prefer to bounce around from thing to thing and work efficiently. As a Manifesting Generator, you are here to be a trailblazer and to push the limits of what is possible. It's important for you to have the freedom to choose diverse ways of using your energy each day and the space in your daily life to play and have fun. That can look like having three projects you are working on while also spending time on four other hobbies!

Because you can have so many different interests, you work quickly, are a fast learner, and almost always feel ready to move on to the next thing. It can be tempting to get ahead of yourself and be thinking ten steps ahead on what you will do in an hour, a day, or next week. You then end up not focused on what is actually in front of you. Slow down and consciously choose to be present with what is in front of you; otherwise, you can miss steps, get frustrated, and have to go back or start again.

Slow down and consciously choose to be present with what is in front of you.

STRATEGY: TO RESPOND

As a Manifesting Generator, your Strategy is to respond (as it would be for a Generator). You are here to use your energy doing what you want to do, and how you discover what you want to do is through responding. The simplest definition of responding is to "act or behave in reaction to something or someone" (according to Oxford Languages). Although this definition works, Man-Gens are not here to respond to life with their mind. Instead, they are here to respond to life with their sacral responses.

A sacral response comes from your sacral center. It is a primal gut response that arises in your lower belly and energizes your body. When you come across something that elicits a positive sacral response, it feels like an ignited energy of desire and excitement in your body that may even be instinctually vocalized as an "ooo" or an "uh-huh, yes!" A positive sacral response is your body's way of telling you that you've come across something you desire and that now is the correct time for you to engage with this thing.

If your sacral center responds to something with a decrease of energy, which may even vocalize as an "uh-uh, no," your body is telling you that you do not desire that thing at this moment and it's not in alignment for you to engage with it right now. This may change in a couple of hours, days, or weeks, but for now, you are not meant to do the thing.

Now, we want to talk about the in between stuff. What if you don't feel anything toward the thing in front of you? That is also your body telling you "no for now." This is the most common thing you might feel, and it is the hardest to say no to. You can easily end up saying yes to mediocre things because they don't result in a strong no, so you can think of reasons why they could be a yes. This is especially true if someone asks something of you (your help with a project, going to lunch, etc.), because you can feel bad and talk yourself into it.

It is so important to say "no for now" to mediocre things. They are actually where you leak your energy the most, and they can cause major burnout in your life. If you are in love with your work or career but feel exhausted all the time, checking in with your body in this way and truly saying "no for now" when you feel nothing can be a major game changer!

Here is what following these sacral responses might look like in real life: Imagine that you're looking at your morning coffee. In the core of your body, do you feel expansive, light, and easy, like you have energy to pour into making this cup of coffee? Or do you feel contraction in your gut, a pit in your stomach, or even the tiniest bit of exhaustion toward it? The expansion and energy are a "yes, now is the time for this coffee in front of me." The contraction and exhaustion are a "no, now is not the time for this coffee in front of me." If it's a no, can you go to the fridge and check in with your body there? Do you have energy to pour into making anything in there? If not, can you step outside and feel whether you have energy to go to a coffee shop? If yes, great! Now is the time to listen to what your body has told you. After following your body's call to engage, you find yourself in the coffee shop, where you overhear a conversation that inspires you to start a new business, project, or idea—or is simply exactly what you needed to hear! You would have missed it if you were at home making your coffee because it's what you "should" do.

The more you can listen to your body in this way, the better. Check in with that contraction or expansion as much as you can and honor it. Of course, there are going to be times when you feel the contraction/exhaustion and you still have to do the thing (otherwise none of us would ever do laundry again), but just noting that you are doing something that your body is not into will still increase your magnetism.

To practice the Strategy of responding in daily life, we like to break it down into asking yourself these three questions:

- "What is directly in front of me right now?"
- "How does my body feel about it?"
- "Can I listen?"

These three questions help you to be fully present with the stimuli in your environment. They also help you quiet your mind's interference so you can listen to your body's internal guidance system. Because you are a Man-Gen, your body is designed to guide you to be in the right place at the right time. As much as our minds might try, they are not connected to divine timing. It is our bodies that are connected to this divine flow.

As a Manifesting Generator, you also have some powerful Manifestor aspects to your energy. Because of this, the way you use your energy each day is very impactful and a bit unpredictable to the people around you. Therefore, a secondary Strategy of informing is also beneficial for you to practice daily. When you have had a sacral response and found clarity on what you want, it is extremely helpful for you to then voice that clarity to the people around you before taking action. If you ever experience resistance from others when you pivot, it is likely because you kept them in the dark and then surprised them with your actions. Informing lets people in on where you are and rallies their support for your endeavors. With this open communication and the support it elicits, you'll experience a greater sense of freedom and peace in your life as you follow your sacral responses.

MAGNETIZING YOUR AURA BY MANAGING YOUR FOREST

You are a magnet. As a Man-Gen, your main priority is to magnetize your aura so life can bring you all of the things you desire. You do this mainly by using your Strategy and by creating space in your day-to-day life. If you are busy all the time and have no open space, there is no room in your energy for something new to be brought to you. When we want change, transition, or just for our dreams to manifest into reality, we need room for something new to come in. We cannot be at capacity.

You are a magnet.

Think of your daily energy usage as a forest full of trees. Each tree represents something you spend your time and energy doing. Some trees are healthy and thriving, while others are lifeless and dying but are still standing there taking up space. When we want change or something new, the first thing we do is plant new seeds everywhere. However, if there is no room for those seeds to take root, they cannot grow. To make space for something new, we must first manage our forest. We do this by assessing the forest, identifying the dead trees, and removing at least one of them to make some open space.

In real life, the process of managing your energetic forest looks like writing a list of all the things you did yesterday. Ask yourself: How many of them felt good and easy to do? How many of them drained you? How many of them did you *have* to do but didn't *want* to? How many of them felt just okay? From there, it's not about removing all the things that drained you, but instead removing just one to create some open space in your day tomorrow. Now, it's crucial that you don't fill that time before it comes. If you now have fifteen minutes or an hour free tomorrow, it is tempting for your mind to say, "I have free time tomorrow. What should I do?! Should I get a massage? Should I take a nap? Should I work out?" Should, should, should. It is important to resist filling that time with anything before it arrives. Instead, use your Strategy to decide how you want to spend that time in the moment when it arrives. Move your body in front of different options (e.g., your bookshelf, fridge, bed, car) and feel in your body what is being ignited. Dedicating this time to listening to your body is the best way to actively increase your magnetism.

SELF THEME AND NOT-SELF THEME

The self themes for Manifesting Generators are satisfaction and peace. When you are in alignment, you are designed to feel completely satisfied with your life in the present moment and like the close people in your life are supportive of your need for freedom. The feeling of satisfaction is the main signpost that you have used up all of your energy for the day in a way that met your desires. Although this is the goal, we live in a world that teaches us that we must spend our energy doing things that we don't want to do. Neglecting your desires in small or big ways and not communicating often can cause you to experience frustration and anger. Your main not-self themes of frustration and anger can feel like intense difficulty and a heated sense of annoyance, or they can feel like a subtle undertone of just being over something and feeling stuck. The two most common causes for misalignment are boredom and getting ahead of yourself, and thus not paying attention to what is actually in front of you.

DAILY PRACTICE

1   **Select an amount of time between two weeks and one month.** Use it to practice asking yourself what is in front of you and how your body feels about it. Can you listen? If not, just take note.

2   **Make a list of all the tasks you do in a day.** Do them while listening to your body and find one you can remove to create open space.

3   **Any time you have open space, wait for that time to arrive** and then check in with your body with whatever is directly in front of you. Move your body around until something in front of you feels expansive and is a yes from your body. Inform the people around you and spend that time doing that thing.

4   **Have others ask you yes-or-no questions.** This makes it easier for you to hear your truth.

5   **Keep people in the loop.** Inform your family, friends, and co-workers about what you're excited to do next or losing interest in.

6   **Allow yourself to release constant "productivity"** and find or cultivate hobbies that feel like play for you. Any time you are feeling bored, make it a priority to do one of these things.

CONDITIONING FOR MANIFESTING GENERATORS

The biggest conditioning Manifesting Generators take on is pressure to be consistent and to work in a linear way. A lot of Man-Gens feel as though they are a "jack of all trades and master of none." Society promotes the belief that consistency leads to success, but that is not how MGs reach success. They reach success by working on things that feel exciting and energizing and by having *a lot* of freedom to shift their focus to a new skill/interest whenever they want to. However, they can feel that if they change their mind or their interests too frequently, they will come off as flaky. The truth is the diverse variety of skills they cultivate end up being transferable, building upon each other and enhancing the next project they take on.

Another form of conditioning that Manifesting Generators (and Generators) face is the expectation that they put their head down and work hard at whatever is asked of them. Because Manifesting Generators are capable, efficient, and have the sacral energy to get things done, their energy can be taken advantage of. There is a misconception that they are here to be the worker bees of the planet. This cannot be further from the truth. Man-Gens are here to work on what they love. Doing so is their soul's mission and their biggest contribution to society. Only when they are doing what they love do they continue to generate a sustainable flow of the sacred life-force energy that nourishes the world around them.

Man-Gens share a lot of conditioning with Generators because their auras operate in a similar way. Other conditioned beliefs can include:

- Your desires make you selfish.
- Things that are exciting or fun are not practical, and you cannot make money doing them.
- It's your job to make sure people feel comfortable all the time.
- You are too much, and you need to dim your light to fit in with others.
- You are not a good student or role model.
- You are not able to focus (a lot of MGs are improperly diagnosed with ADHD).

MANIFESTING GENERATORS IN LIFE

Work

Freedom, play, flexibility, and variety are key themes for any Manifesting Generator when it comes to work. Some Man-Gens have two or three careers at once. Having the freedom to choose what they are working on and when allows them to flow from one thing to the next and is actually the most efficient use of their time. If they are forced to work a 9-to-5 job doing the same thing every day, they will eventually feel bogged down, trapped, and stuck in their life. Ultimately, it is important that they get to spend their energy working on things that they love doing.

Physical Body and Sleep

For Man-Gens, having an hour to wind down before bed is ideal. It's imperative that they use all of their energy up each day. This helps them avoid any stuck energy that can create restlessness, anxiety, or even depression. Cultivating physical activities that are new, exciting, or challenging can be a great way to expel any leftover energy they may have. When it comes to food and diet, the best diet is one that they choose for themselves. They may find that they need to consume more food than others to maintain a healthy energy level.

Children

Making time for play, variety, and creativity is the best way to support a Man-Gen child. Allowing them to try many different things and quit if they are bored or dislike it is ideal. Man-Gen children move quickly, so offering an environment where this is allowed while encouraging them to slow down when they feel frustrated creates a safe space for them to explore who they are. As a parent, the more you can inform them of what you are doing, thinking, planning, and feeling, the more you will lead by example and teach them to do the same. This prevents the feeling of whiplash some parents can have when unaware of what their Man-Gen child wants to do next.

Relationships

Man-Gens need to be loved in a way in which they feel free—free to be who they are and free to explore what they want, whenever they want. Desire is a huge theme in relationships for Man-Gens. For them to enter into a new romantic partnership correctly, they must have a feeling of embodied energetic desire for the other person. Selecting a romantic partner with their desire over "what makes sense" and initiating the relationship will set them up for a healthy partnership.

Manifesting Generator Not-Self Theme Quiz

Select the answer that best describes your current feelings. **Keep track of how many As, Bs, and Cs you select.**

My relationship to my family and other close supportive relationships:

A I often find myself feeling pressure to stick to things I have started even when I am over them so that what I am doing makes sense to my family. I feel pressure to be responsible by their standards and use my capabilities to help them, and I feel guilty when I create time for myself to indulge in the things that I want to do.

B I'm getting better at saying no when I'm not actually lit up by helping, although I'm not perfect at it. At first it felt scary to let myself be playful, expansive, and free, but now I'm finding that doing so helps me have more energy, space, and clarity about the ways I want to help my loved ones.

C I only help out or give when I genuinely want to for the most part. As I follow my own path with love and curiosity, I notice how much my energy expands into my family. As I deepen my acceptance of myself and my path, I notice my family does as well.

My relationship to my career/ life purpose:

A I definitely don't feel lit up or energized by what I'm currently doing, but I also have no idea what I would want to be doing instead. I feel stuck where I currently am, but I get confused and overwhelmed when I even think about phasing out of it and starting something new.

B I am lit up about parts of what I am currently doing. However, I do feel bored and limited within certain aspects.

C I can honestly say that I love what I do. It feels good to get to show up and pour my creativity into building, playing, and working in a diverse and freeing way. I feel present and energized when I am engaged with all the different facets of my work.

My relationship to my energy levels and physical well-being:

A I often feel dull, stuck, and like my energy is unfocused, not wanting to work on anything in particular. I can have too much unsettled energy to fall asleep or feel a lack of energy in the morning.

B I'm finding that through giving myself permission to do less of what I'm no longer into and more of what I am lit up by, I feel more energized, playful, and expansive overall.

C I feel guided by my sacral responses about how to nourish my body in every moment. By the end of the day, I've used up all of my energy and I give myself time to transition into bedtime feeling fulfilled. Each morning I wake up with a fresh tank of energy, excited to discover what a new day will bring me.

My relationship to my romantic partner(s):

A I often feel like I over-give to my partner or force myself to be consistent by trying to be what they need me to be. I have to dim my light to fit into the confinements of my relationship.

B I am starting to honor myself and my needs more. I notice that the more connected I am to my sense of play and joy, the deeper, more nourishing, and more exciting my relationships feel.

C My romantic partnership is full of depth, freedom, clear communication, and healthy boundaries. I feel encouraged to follow my joy and also feel supported in saying no when I want to. My relationship helps me to be even more in tune with my body.

My relationship with myself:

A I don't really know what's special about myself, what I'm into, or where I belong. I'm feeling a bit lost at the moment. I'm afraid that I'll never find my way.

B I feel like I've begun finding who I am through paying attention to the things my body responds to. I still get hung up on questioning where my future will lead me at times, but overall I am discovering where I want to go and how I'm meant to use my gifts in this world through discovering what lights me up and prioritizing more play.

C I fully appreciate the fact that I am a creative and capable being and that I am here to be expansive and build anything I want to in this lifetime. I see how easily I connect with people, bring people together, and inspire others. I love that all I have to do to use my energy correctly is follow my sacral responses.

MOSTLY AS: LIVING IN YOUR NOT-SELF

If you answered mostly As, you may be living in your not-self more often than not. You may be feeling frustrated and angry quite frequently because you have been using your energy doing what others think you should do instead of what you actually want to do.

The more you focus on being present and listening to what your body responds to with energy and excitement, the more you will be guided toward where to correctly spend your energy. This will lead you back to your natural aligned state of satisfaction. Following your sacral responses may sound simple, but it is no easy feat with the way we are conditioned to work and show up for other people. Remember to bring your awareness to the present moment when you catch yourself feeling frustrated. It is easier to release the pressure to be linear and lean in to curiosity, fun, and exploration when you remember that you are always being led by your inner compass with your sacral responses.

MOSTLY BS: GROWING IN THE RIGHT DIRECTION

If you answered mostly Bs, you are finding your flow around living in personal alignment. There may be moments where you still feel frustrated, and that's okay! It's all about having awareness of your not-self and letting it prompt you back to being present, managing your forest, and responding.

You are beginning to prove to yourself that the more you embrace your multifaceted, multi-passionate nature by following what lights you up, the more you magnetically attract the right opportunities, inspirations, and connections that bring you so much satisfaction.

MOSTLY CS: SATISFIED EXPANSIVE BEING

If you answered mostly Cs, you are mostly living in personal alignment! You are experiencing life as a flowing, free, lit-up Manifesting Generator who exudes the powerful life-force energy that the world needs from you.

Remember that even when you are aligned, and you feel satisfied with how you are spending your energy each day, your inner guidance only really operates in the present. We invite you to lean in to trusting your body's wisdom, trusting that you are a magnetic being, and trusting that the inspiration and opportunities about what's next will find you.

TIPS AND RECOMMENDATIONS FOR LIVING YOUR DESIGN

Tips

- SING IN THE CAR OR SHOWER to open up your throat chakra to free your sacral sounds.
- SIMPLIFY YOUR OPTIONS when making small decisions so you can more easily hear your truth.
- SLOW DOWN THROUGHOUT THE DAY to check in with your body.
- SAY ALOUD THREE INTENTIONS you have for the day every morning.
- SAY ALOUD THREE THINGS you are grateful for every evening.
- SAY THE MANTRA, "When I am present, I always know what to do."

Supportive Crystals

- ORANGE CALCITE for creative energy
- GREEN JASPER for presence and grounding
- CITRINE for increasing confidence and magnetism
- BLACK TOURMALINE for cleansing conditioning
- AMAZONITE for clear communication
- CARNELIAN for fertile new growth

Essential Oils

- CINNAMON
- ORANGE BLOSSOM
- LAVENDER
- CHAMOMILE
- PEPPERMINT

Meditations

- **LET YOUR BODY GUIDE YOU TO AN ESSENTIAL OIL** it wants to receive. Breathe in the aroma and describe the energetic shifts you feel in your body.
- **DO AN EMBODIMENT MEDITATION** by playing music that captures your current mood and dancing, stretching, or moving your body in a way that feels good.
- **TURN A MUNDANE TASK INTO A PRESENCE RITUAL** by focusing on deeply observing every physical sensation you have while doing the task.
- **WATCH AN ONLINE VIDEO ON BREATH OF FIRE BREATHING.** Set a timer and do this intense breathwork for three minutes to clear stuck energy.

DECONDITIONING JOURNAL PROMPTS

- **Do I have trouble saying no to people?**
- **Do I feel I often miss steps** and need to slow down more in life?
- **How do I feel in my body when I slow down?**
- **How do I feel when others tell me what to do?**
- **Do I have any relationships in which I often feel resistance** or misunderstood? How can I lean in to informing and communicating more openly with those people?
- **In what areas of my life do I lack freedom?** How do I feel about it?
- **Do I feel that my needs or desires are selfish** or unimportant?
- **How can I allow others to help me more?**
- **Do I have activities or hobbies that I love** and that feel playful for me? How often do I allow myself time to do them?
- **What is something I am currently doing every day** (in work or in my personal life) that I can cut out to make space in my day?
- **In what areas of my life am I holding back** because I'm afraid of change?
- **List ten things you love about yourself.** Now say them out loud.
- **List ten things you love about the people in your life.** Now say them out loud.

Projectors

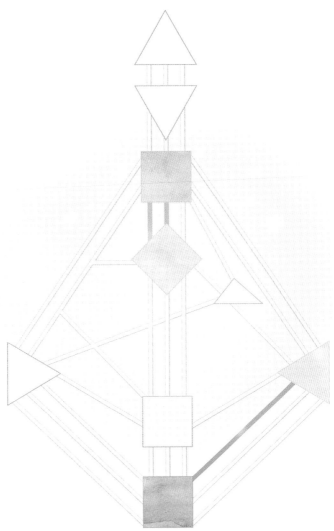

QUICK FACTS

- **AURA:** Penetrating and Focused
- **STRATEGY:** Wait For the Invitation
- **SELF THEME:** Success

- **NOT-SELF THEME:** Bitterness
- **HERE TO:** Guide Others and Make Life More Efficient

Projectors

Projectors comprise around 20 percent of the population.

As a Projector, you operate differently than the majority of people in your life. While the major energetic contribution of the other Types is in what they do, create, or build, your energy is here to contribute what you see and to help guide the energy use of others.

Your aura is penetrating and focused, meaning when you are around other people, your energy actually reaches into the other person to see them. Because of the way your aura exchanges energy, you are gifted at recognizing and identifying what makes people special. You can also see how they can make changes or corrections to become a more authentic version of themselves. Not only can you dive into people, but you can also dive into systems, processes, projects, and businesses. When you look into a system, you can see what needs to be shifted to help the process become optimized through efficiency.

Because Projectors do not have their sacral center defined, they are considered non-energy beings. Without a consistent sacral motor fueling you each day, you are designed to have an inconsistent flow of energy in your body. Depending on the day and whom you're around, you can have more or less energy. It is healthy for you to only work around two to four hours a day on tasks that make you feel like you are expending energy. Spend the rest of your time resting or working on things that are interesting and effortless for you. This can also look like working really hard for a couple of days and then taking the rest of the week to rest. Although it is the status quo in our culture to work eight hours a day, five days a week, this schedule is not sustainable for Projectors. Consistently working more than two to four hours a day will eventually result in burnout and can even lead to major health issues. You are not here to "do" in the same way other people are. Your energetic body is designed to achieve success by using your inconsistent energy levels to work smarter, not harder. As a Projector, if you do not prioritize rest, then you will never reach the amount of success you are here to achieve.

Even though your energy is inconsistent, there are many benefits to being a Projector. You have a unique way of seeing the world and the people in it, and others look to you for your insight and guidance. Every Projector has their own niche or special area of genius. Whether yours is in the way you understand human behavior, parenting, human resources, or interior design, there is something that you see in a way that others simply can't. Your insight in this particular area and your advice (when solicited) is incredibly valuable to the world around you. Reframing how you feel about work is important: You are not here to trade your time for money. Instead, you are here to trade your wisdom for money.

> You are not here to trade your time for money. Instead, you are here to trade your wisdom for money.

When a Projector has fully honed their unique genius in their particular realm of expertise, they can share one valuable idea with a client and earn as much as they would working a full eight-hour shift in a random job. Projectors are not limited in what they can do or what field they work in. If they are able to share their valuable insight, they can do anything they want. As a Projector, you are here to spend your time focusing on what truly fascinates you. These fascinations will lead to ideas and creations from which you can guide others, whether you are doing that from the position of CEO, writer, life coach, artist, or something else.

There are three categories of Projectors:

Energy Projector: This Projector has one or more of three motor centers (root, solar plexus, or ego) defined. They have a bit more energy to do than other Projectors. They have a tendency to overwork themselves.

Classic Projector: This Projector has no motors centers (root, solar plexus, or ego) defined, but has definition under the Throat center. They are designed to be the most discerning of whose energy they want to be around.

Energy Projector   Classic Projector   Mental Projector

Mental Projector: This Projector has only the head, ajna, or throat center defined. They have no definition below the throat center. They are deeply influenced by the environments they spend time in. They can have the most conditioning of all the Projectors. They have a strong intellect that provides deep value to the world.

STRATEGY: TO WAIT FOR THE INVITATION

As a Projector, your Strategy in life is to wait for the invitation. This means allowing other people to come to you and ask you for your advice and guidance. Yes, you have an uncanny ability to see people clearly and know what they need. But if they have not given you consent to look inside their lives and tell them how they can improve their situation, then your advice is going to offend and repel rather than be appreciated.

So, what does an invitation look like? A proper invitation is comprised of three parts:

1   **The recipient recognizes you** for your talent and wisdom.

2   **They verbally ask you for your advice** or guidance or energetically show a clear interest.

3   **You feel there is space for your advice,** guidance, talent, or insight to land and truly be received.

For example, someone might ask you for your advice, but you can tell that they are not actually open to what you have to say. That is not an invitation. Someone else might ask for your guidance and you can feel that they really value your opinion. That is an invitation. Someone else may not verbally ask for your advice, but when they talk about their problem, you can sense they want and are ready to receive advice from you. This would be an energetic invitation. Let's say you receive an email from someone who saw your resume and thinks you would be an amazing asset to their team. That is an invitation. Someone else could see your resume and ask if you wouldn't mind learning a new skill or doing another job within their team that you don't really love. That is not a healthy invitation.

Recognition is the most important part of the invitation. If someone is randomly asking for your advice or skills, but you don't feel like they really want it or that they don't actually value your gifts, then it is not an aligned invitation for you. It is important to wait for a proper invitation; otherwise, your gifts are going to fall flat and you will be left feeling unrecognized and bitter.

To be clear, you do not need to wait for an invitation to talk about the things you love or find interesting in your own life! It is good for you to talk about yourself and why you love what you love; that is how people see and recognize you. It is only when you are giving someone else advice about their life that you need to be invited. It's important not to say, "You should try this" or "This worked for me, so it will work for you too because we have the same problem" without a proper invitation.

We like to break waiting for the invitation into two sections:

1 **Your Personal Life:** This can look like biting your tongue sometimes and not giving your advice even though you know it would really help someone. That means not saying to your best friend that maybe all her ex-boyfriends have been toxic because she has low self-worth (harsh) and instead waiting for her to come to you when she is ready.

2 **Your Career and Life Purpose:** This is where waiting for the invitation looks completely different. When it comes to your career, you are designed to build it, share it, and *let people come to you.* You do not need an invitation to start your own business, project, or product or to hire employees. In fact, if that is what is fascinating to you, you should! You just should not be reaching out to customers or clients and asking them whether they want to buy your product—that would be repelling. Instead, it is best to post, "Here is this thing I've created. This is why I love it and why it is so fascinating to me! Here is a link if you want to join." In this way, you are not saying "you should buy it"; you are sharing your offerings. Anyone who goes to your website, follows your page, or similar has invited you.

So, what do you do while you are waiting for the invitations to come in? Waiting for an invitation does not mean sitting at home all day watching movies. This is the time to hone your skills and increase your magnetism. Read books, watch documentaries, take a class, and spend time focusing on things that fascinate you. Your focus is your greatest asset and superpower. Whatever you focus on, you create magnetism around. You will eventually start to see invitations rolling in. If your focus is all over the place and swept up in your day-to-day life, you will be creating magnetism that is scattered and not directed at anything specific. Similarly, if your focus is on the things that you don't love about your life, you will be creating magnetism around those things, and they will get worse. That is the last place you want to direct your superpower. Redirect your focus to the things that you love about your life.

Whatever you focus on, you create magnetism around.

MAGNETIZING YOUR AURA BY BUILDING YOUR LIGHTHOUSE

For a moment, think of the other Types in Human Design as boats on the water. They have a consistent sacral engine to keep them going all day long, but they are down in the water, and they can only see what is directly in front of them. As a Projector, you are not a boat; you are a lighthouse. You are not designed to be down in the water. Instead, it is your job to build your lighthouse tall and shine your light. So, how do you do that? You build your lighthouse brick by brick by knowing your gifts, focusing on what fascinates you, getting clear on what you want to share, building an offering or a business, and resting when you need to. Then it is time to shine your light!

Shining your light is a big step that a lot of Projectors miss. It looks like having a website or social media, or talking about what you love with friends and family. If you do not share/shine your light, how are boats supposed to follow you? You are a lighthouse! It is not your job to figure out which boats are going to follow you or whether they will want to follow you. Your focus should be in building yourself up and shining just for the sake of shining.

Although Projectors see well into others, they too often give their power away when they focus on what other people think of them or whether they will (or will not) be recognized or invited. Projectors tend to have a blindspot when it comes to seeing themselves, so a great shift of personal empowerment happens for them when they turn their powerful focus inward toward themselves. We like the analogy of building your lighthouse and shining your light because it helps you to stop seeking recognition from outside sources and start recognizing yourself. Once you start building yourself up brick by brick, you increase your magnetism and visibility so others can actually see you and invite you.

Once you've built your lighthouse and gotten clear on something you want invitations for (business, new offering, specific job, etc.), there are three questions you can ask yourself:

1   **Am I focused on it?** This does not have to be all-day focus; it can be as simple as fifteen minutes in meditation envisioning what you want it to look like.

2   **Can people see me?** Is there a place (website, social media, conversations with friends and family, etc.) for people to see you focused on this thing?

3   **Am I being authentic?** As a Projector, your authenticity is your key to success. If you are sharing something because you can't help but sing it from the mountaintops, people will flock to it because your authenticity is so attractive.

DAILY PRACTICE

1   **Ask yourself, "What fascinates me today?"** and spend time doing that thing.

2   **Allow your fascinations to shift and change.** You don't need to try to control or limit them so that they make sense to your mind. Instead, focus on being authentic with what is truly fascinating to you without judgment.

3   **Only work hard for two to four hours** each day. Set a timer if it helps.

4   **Prioritize rest and listen to your body** when it says you need a break.

5   **Wait for the invitation before giving direct advice,** and freely share yourself and what fascinates you in spaces where you don't need an invitation.

When you first hear that your Strategy is to wait for the invitation, you might feel disempowered. But as you can see, you are completely empowered to build your life. Waiting for the invitation is not a passive thing, but rather a beautiful way of being that attracts your dreams to you in a way that actually serves you.

SELF THEME AND NOT-SELF THEME

The self theme for Projectors is success, meaning that you are meant to experience success in this lifetime in all the things that you do! This is why many Projectors are obsessed with their careers even though the way they are designed to work doesn't fit into the standard eight-hour workday that our society has deemed a prerequisite for success. When you are in alignment, you are designed to feel successful with your life, your work, your projects, and your relationships and in all the other small ways you receive recognition. This also means that when you are operating in alignment, you will see tangible financial success as well as appreciation and recognition on the emotional/spiritual plane. A feeling of success is a signpost that you have been getting to guide others in a way that was fascinating for you and that you honored your energy when it was time to rest. Although it is the goal to embody your self theme, it's easy to fall out of alignment when you exhaust yourself or operate outside of your design. This is when you can experience your not-self theme of bitterness. Bitterness is a strong feeling that things are unfair. You can feel jealous, overlooked, or misunderstood. The most common causes of misalignment for Projectors are overworking and feeling a lack of recognition.

CONDITIONING FOR PROJECTORS

The main conditioning you can take on as a Projector is the belief that you have to work hard to be successful. Society is constantly telling us to put in long hours, hustle, and grind, and that only those who are consistent make it to the top. This conditioning leads to a lot of Projectors operating as if they were Manifesting Generators and then working the hardest out of any of their coworkers. If this sounds like you, there is a reason! You are gifted at seeing how things can be made better and what needs to be done, so instead of just giving that advice and going home, you end up doing it all. You handle everything and are a super-efficient go-getter, but at the end of the day you are exhausted . . . and over time, burnt out. You are meant to see all of those efficiency gains; however, you are not meant to implement them all yourself.

The other biggest conditioning you can fall victim to is the belief that you need to physically match everyone else and that resting is lazy. Society leads us to believe that every moment needs to be productive and that if you cannot keep up with those around you, you are lazy. This is a big idea you will need to reframe. For Projectors, rest is productive. The more rest you allow yourself, the more success you will experience in your life. That sounds too good to be true, but once you start experimenting with your design, you will begin to prove it to yourself!

Other conditioned beliefs can include:

- You have to force things to happen or they never will.
- You are bossy.
- You are a know-it-all.
- Your insight isn't valuable.
- No one wants to hear what you have to share.

PROJECTORS IN LIFE

Work

Projectors are designed to work two to four hours a day with a hard output and then spend the rest of their time working on things that truly fascinate them. It is ideal for them to be in a working environment where they feel recognized and can share their insight, guidance, and management skills.

Projectors are excellent self-starters, and working for themselves can allow the freedom they need to work efficiently and prioritize rest; however, many successful Projectors work in companies in management positions and can structure breaks and free time in between meetings. To start making a career change to honor their energy, we recommend Projectors take an honest look at what tasks feel like "work" and what tasks feel interesting or fun. Budgeting the hard work for two to four hours each day will make a huge difference in their magnetism and will help attract recognition for what they actually enjoy doing.

Physical Body and Sleep

For Projectors, going to bed before they are exhausted and having an hour alone to clear out and wind down before going to sleep is best. Projectors may find that in general, they need more sleep than other people (eight to ten hours a night is ideal) and that they sleep best when sleeping alone. Although exercise and movement are beneficial for all of thc Types, overdoing it or forcing a workout can have adverse effects on a Projector's well-being. It's best for them to tune in to what feels good to their physical body each day and take cues from that. When it comes to diet, eating large meals can bog down their energy. Light snacking throughout the day and eating lighter at mealtimes can help Projectors keep their energy levels up.

Children

Inviting Projector children to share their insight or guidance is one of the best ways you can recognize them for their gifts and support them in seeing themselves more. Giving them meaningful compliments on their qualities and insights instead of for their physical achievements will help them find value in themselves. The most supportive thing you can do for Projector children is listen to them and encourage rest when they may be pushing themselves too hard.

Relationships

Projectors are meant to be invited into healthy relationships. This can be tricky with our common conditioning around gender roles (for Projector men, for example); however, fully feeling seen and invited by your romantic partner is key. Words of affirmations and meaningful compliments are powerful in supporting your Projector partner. So is asking them for their genuine insight and guidance. It is important that Projectors are not forced to keep up with their partner or have unrealistic expectations set on them to keep going when they need rest.

Projector Not-Self Theme Quiz:

Select the answer that best describes your current feelings. **Keep track of how many As, Bs, and Cs you select.**

My relationship to my family and other close supportive relationships:

A   I often find myself giving people close to me advice that they never take. I can clearly see what is needed, but no one seems to value my opinion. I feel annoyed that my family and close friends don't see me or value my gifts.

B   I'm getting better at releasing the need to always share my insight or advice with people close to me. I am starting to see how much better I feel when I just relax into letting them do their own thing and letting them come to me when they feel ready to hear my advice. However, it's still hard sometimes to feel a bit unseen by them.

C   I love that I get to infuse my wisdom into all areas of my own life. I love when my family and friends come to me when they want my insight, but I'm totally fine when they don't. Actively focusing on loving and recognizing myself has made all of my family relationships and close friendships feel much more harmonious.

My relationship to my career/life purpose:

A   I definitely don't feel recognized in my current position. I feel like I have taken on a role that I am good at but don't love. Honestly, I'm feeling really burnt out.

B   The aspects of my current career in which I get to guide others and improve things in the way I want to are the parts I love. However, there are other parts of my job that really drain me, and I feel they are a waste of my time and energy.

C   I love what I do and the way I get to help guide in my work. I feel like I get to show up as my full self. I feel successful, I feel well compensated for my time, and I feel free to choose the amount of time I work and rest.

My relationship to my energy levels and physical well-being:

A   I almost always feel a complete lack of energy, but I have no idea where I would find the time or space to rest. Every morning I must push myself to get going. I don't really see how it would be possible to do all the things I am responsible for and work less.

B I'm starting to embrace that I am not designed to work the way the world tells me I should. Just having that awareness feels freeing to me. I am choosing to rest in small ways and putting less pressure on myself to keep up with others, but I still feel guilty or unproductive at times when I am trying to scale back on working.

C I have fully given myself permission to work in the way that feels most natural for me. I have completely released comparing what my body needs to what may be right for other people. My days feel spacious, and I trust my body to tell me how much work, rest, exercise, and sleep is right for me.

My relationship to my romantic partner(s):

A I crave to be seen and understood on a deeper level than my partner currently does. I feel like my partner expects so much of me, and I try to always be helpful and supportive of their path, but I don't feel they reciprocate.

B I am spending more time on giving myself the love, encouragement, and recognition I crave. Since doing so, I feel less pressure on my relationship and more ease, flow, and harmony.

C My romantic partnership is a safe space, full of depth and genuine love. I feel that my partner and I really understand each other, see what's special about each other, and encourage each other to be who we want to be in the world.

My relationship with myself:

A I struggle deep down with feeling like I am wasting my true potential. I swing back and forth between feeling pressure to prove myself and feeling like I just don't fit into this world. I feel like I'm here to do big things, but right now it seems like no one really cares about what I have to offer.

B I have really shifted my focus to understanding and honoring my energy and appreciating my gifts, abilities, and insight. It feels good to start seeing myself more clearly and knowing that I am designed to operate differently than the rest of the world. I am really enjoying the process of diving into what fascinates me, even if I'm not sure yet where my fascinations are leading me.

C I can genuinely say that I love being myself and find that I naturally shine my light in my own unique way. I truly recognize the value and worth of my perspective and gifts and feel so blessed to be using my gifts in a way that is fascinating for me. While I am still evolving and expanding, I also feel successful, recognized, and appreciated where I currently am.

MOSTLY AS: LIVING IN YOUR NOT-SELF

If you answered mostly As, you may be living in your not-self more often than not. You may be feeling frequent bitterness around not feeling appreciated or overworking in a way that drains you. This may be because you have been trying to push yourself to work like a Manifesting Generator instead of honoring your true Projector nature.

Remember that the more you start finding ways to scale back on overextending your energy, the more space you will have to start discovering and honing your Projector genius. Although it might seem difficult to trust that the less you test the limits of your energy the more success you will magnetize, it is the truth for you. Remember to be gentle on yourself and give yourself love through nourishing your rest. From a well-rested space, recognizing yourself feels so much easier.

MOSTLY BS: GROWING IN THE RIGHT DIRECTION

If you answered mostly Bs, you are finding your flow around living in personal alignment. There may be moments where you still feel bitterness, and that's okay! It's all about having awareness of when that not-self shows up and letting it prompt you to come back to resting more and recognizing yourself more.

You are beginning to prove to yourself that the more you focus on seeing yourself and building yourself up, the more you receive recognition and magnetize success into your life.

MOSTLY CS: SUCCESSFUL GUIDE

If you answered mostly Cs, you are mostly living in the realm of personal alignment! For the most part, you are experiencing life as a rested, interested, successful Projector who can point others toward authenticity and alignment.

Remember that as you shine your light, receive delicious new invitations to share your wisdom, and step into your highest potential as a guide, it's always about knowing that your value is not meant to be found in how hard you work, but instead in how well you see.

TIPS AND RECOMMENDATIONS FOR LIVING YOUR DESIGN

Tips

- GIVE YOURSELF DAILY COMPLIMENTS. Say them out loud until it doesn't feel weird anymore.
- ASK YOURSELF, "WHAT FASCINATES ME TODAY?" and spend time researching or sharing that thing.
- SET A TIMER FOR TWO TO FOUR HOURS for your hard work output each day and see whether you can stick to that.
- AS AN ACT OF SELF-CARE, START SAYING NO MORE to invitations from friends who drain you, regardless of FOMO.

Supportive Crystals

- LABRADORITE for enhancing insight
- AMETHYST for elevating your perspective
- BLACK OBSIDIAN for releasing bitterness
- BLUE LACE AGATE for promoting relaxation and relieving fatigue
- FLUORITE for helping with focus

Essential Oils

- SANDALWOOD
- MYRRH
- FRANKINCENSE
- ROSE

Meditations

- **FIND A 5 RHYTHMS DANCING PLAYLIST** on Spotify or YouTube. Follow the suggested movements spoken in the songs to help you release stuck energy, bitterness, and judgment of yourself and others.
- **TAKE A NOURISHING BATH** for the hour before bed. Set the intention for self-nourishment by creating an altar on your countertop with candles, flowers, and/or crystals.
- **PRACTICE LYING DOWN TO REST AS A MEDITATION** in inherent self-worth. While you are lying there, feel how precious and valuable your life is, even when you aren't doing anything. If guilt for resting comes in, bathe yourself in white light, washing it away.

DECONDITIONING JOURNAL PROMPTS

- **Where in my life do I feel inferior to others or bitter?**

- **What is fascinating to me right now?**

- **What do I feel like I am getting the most recognition** for right now with work?

- **What do I feel like I am getting the most recognition** for right now with my family/loved ones?

- **Is there anyone in my life who doesn't really see me?** Why is that?

- **How can I focus on seeing myself more** in this area of my life?

- **How am I currently prioritizing rest?**

- **When do I have the most energy?** What does that tell me about my fascinations?

- **What unique insight or observations** have I had recently?

- **How do I feel about being seen** and sharing myself online? How can I explore more ways of being seen?

Reflectors

QUICK FACTS

- **AURA:** Sampling and Resistant
- **STRATEGY:** Wait a Lunar Cycle
- **SELF THEME:** Surprise
- **NOT-SELF THEME:** Disappointment

- **HERE TO:** Amplify Others' Energy and Have Discernment Between What Is and Is Not Healthy Or Working

Reflectors

Reflectors are the rarest of the five types, comprising approximately only 1 percent of the population.

The Reflector aura is sampling and resistant. As a Reflector, you are designed to empathetically take in the energy of others and temporarily experience an amplified version of their energy in your own body. Your aura can also resist taking in energy that doesn't feel good to you. In this respect, your aura helps protect you from picking up too much conditioning from the world around you. The people you spend time with can see themselves reflected in your energy when they are with you. Because you mirror back their energy, they can see what is in alignment within themselves and what is not.

All Reflectors have a completely undefined chart, with no centers defined (colored in). This means that on your own, you have a clear, open, non-obtrusive presence. Without a defined sacral, you are a considered a non-energy being. You do not have your own consistent source of energy but can be fueled by an amplified version of the energy you've picked up from others. You, more than any other Type, are truly designed to be a vessel, a clear container that can fill up with the energy of the world around you and then empty out. Because of this complete openness, Reflectors can experience the widest range of human behavior and can have the most wisdom and understanding of any of the Types. Your rare energy makes you sensitive and profoundly empathetic. Because so much of your experience on a day-to-day basis depends on whom you are around and what energy you take in and temporarily become, each day brings a new surprise. You are designed to wake up each day and ask yourself, "Who am I today?"

The four other Types are considered solar beings, as they are deeply connected to and impacted by the energy of the sun. As a Reflector, you are the only Type that is considered a lunar being, meaning that not only are you conditioned daily by the people around you, but you are also conditioned by the energy of the moon. Every day, as the moon orbits our planet, it shifts through different gates that cause it to carry and transmit different energetic qualities. You take in and experience these lunar qualities inside your energetic field. Throughout an entire twenty-eight-day lunar cycle, the moon will have made a transit through all 64 of the Human Design gates. When you ask yourself, "Who am I today?" you are not only asking, "What energy have I picked up from the people I have been around?" but also "What lunar energy have I picked up and experienced within myself?"

Although your energy is meant to change and shift each day, your Profile, Gates, and Cross of Incarnation are consistent qualities for you and can help give you a greater sense of self.

STRATEGY: TO WAIT FOR A LUNAR CYCLE

As a Reflector, your Strategy is to wait a twenty-eight-day lunar cycle. With the moon transiting through the totality of the 64 gates in a lunar cycle, you will have experienced all of those different energies reflected within yourself as well. While the moon is in Gate 8 (a quality of sharing your creative eye), you will feel more creative. While the moon is in Gate 4 (a quality of creating logical solutions), you will feel more logical. Depending on the gates you have in your own chart, you may even temporarily experience having a defined mind or a defined solar plexus, causing you to fixate on a certain perspective or experience random emotions (having a temporary emotional wave). The way you and the moon move through these gates is a consistent and repetitive cycle that happens approximately each month/lunar cycle. As the qualities of all the different gates pop up in your field for you to experience and then release, you will feel different levels and layers of your truth being illuminated with you. Only when the entire cycle comes to completion will you have accessed all facets of feeling your truth within yourself.

To move through life with the most ease and alignment, it's important to wait out an entire lunar cycle before making a big change. Intently observing how you feel each day with each new gate temporarily illuminated within you helps you have more depth and confidence in discovering your own feelings of what is right or not right for your life path. As a Reflector, you will automatically have Lunar Authority as your decision-making process. (To learn more about how to make decisions, head to the Lunar Authority section.)

Giving yourself an entire month to receive clarity about how you feel might sound like too much. It is, after all, more than we are usually given to make a decision by our boss, our doctor, or even our partner. It might seem impossible to actually start living this way, considering the modern world is all about the go-go-go hustle. However, in all honesty, the biggest hurdle to experimenting with this Strategy is actually yourself. Once you decide you are ready to start creating the space needed to honor this time frame, you will see how much it can change your life. Waiting a lunar cycle allows you to connect more deeply to the sacred cycles of nature meant to guide you. It connects you to the divine timing life is wanting to support you with, and it is the only true way to access your aligned clarity.

Waiting a lunar cycle to make a decision allows you to connect more deeply to the sacred cycles of nature.

MAGNETIZING YOUR AURA BY CLEARING OUT YOUR VESSEL

As a Reflector, you are here to be everything and nothing. You are here to taste test an unlimited number of experiences, feelings, interests, and qualities in this lifetime. Although these experiences fill you up, none of them define you. You are not meant to be defined by anything in this lifetime. You are here to be an expansive vessel.

Think of your energy like the sky: sacred, spacious, and open.

When a rainstorm passes through the sky, the sky welcomes the storm. It holds the storm in all its magnificence. The sky is a vessel that fills up with and is completely colored by the storm. The storm expands, shifts, and roars within the space of the sky. Then it passes, and the sky is still there—clear, open, and expansive.

Next, a beautiful, golden sunset appears, filling up the sky. The sky holds its color, its vibrancy, and its glow. The sky has now become completely characterized by the sunset's beauty and light. And then the sunset passes, the colors fade, and the sky is still there—a clear, open vessel.

As a Reflector, you are the sky. You are here to openly allow new weather to come in, color your energy body, feel that weather as an experience, amplify the depth and beauty of it, and then clear out and let it go.

We love this analogy because it helps you see yourself as the expansive, sacred being you are. True magic happens when you fully lean in to learning and evolving from each new experience, person, lunar transit, and interest that comes into your realm without feeling the need to hold on to it or try to define yourself by it.

It is not the passing weather that defines you. You are the undefinable, ever-changing sky.

DAILY PRACTICE

1 Ask yourself, **"Who am I today?"** and allow yourself to be open to feeling different things throughout the day.

2 **At the end of each day, journal one sentence** about how you felt that day (creative, emotional, energized, tired, motivated, etc.).

3 **Actively release what you are feeling** and choose to clear out with your awareness.

4 **Spend time in the environments** where you feel the most healthy and authentic.

SELF THEME AND NOT-SELF THEME

The self theme for Reflectors is surprise. When you are in alignment and allow yourself to show up each day with an openness and receptivity to whatever and wherever life leads you next, you embody a state of childlike wonder and playfulness. This feeling of surprise, lightness, delight, and awe at the endless potential, possibility, and depth of life is a signpost that you have been successfully clearing out and letting yourself flow without attachment. It's easy to fall out of alignment when you try to force consistency in your energy or interests. It is from this place of misalignment that you will experience your not-self theme of disappointment.

To a Reflector, disappointment can feel like something you thought was true about yourself or your life path that ended up not being real. That hobby you really wanted to be your thing no longer feels right. That person you felt so similar to or connected with now feels completely different. These letdowns about circumstances and people moving on can leave you with an overall disheartened perspective on life in general. Living in a state of disappointment as a Reflector can make every new day feel meaningless and chaotic instead of joyful, surprising, and adventurous.

CONDITIONING FOR REFLECTORS

The main conditioning you can take on as a Reflector is the idea that you need to hide or ignore your sensitivity. In general, our societal conditioning does not value being sensitive, open, and empathetic. Reflectors can be taught from a young age to hide and/or ignore how impacted they are by the health and well-being of the world around them. They are taught to stifle the discernment their body feels, charge forward, and distract themselves by staying busy. Because of this conditioning, Reflectors can live their whole life feeling like their empathy is their greatest weakness, when in fact it is their greatest strength.

Another aspect of conditioning Reflectors face is the pressure to force themselves to have distinguishable and unchanging qualities. Society puts an overemphasis on being consistent and having a strong, assertive, and distinctive presence. Reflectors are here to allow their interests to flow as freely as life itself. The people they come into contact with introduce them to new things, and they move on when it feels natural. Their own characteristics are also meant to be in a constant state of flux as they mirror and amplify the people they spend time with and the ever-shifting cosmic energy. Their conditioning leads Reflectors to believe that if they allow themselves to be inconsistent, they will always be lost. The truth is the opposite: When Reflectors flow freely without holding back, they find their joy and purpose.

Other conditioned beliefs can include:

- Feeling left out or invisible
- Not knowing who you are or overidentifying with things that you come across
- Feeling pressure to choose who you are or what you want in life
- Feeling you cannot be successful if you are not consistent and hustling
- Feeling lazy or not enough
- Always feeling behind or rushed through your process

REFLECTORS IN LIFE

Work

Reflectors can work in any job they feel has a healthy, fun, and expansive social and physical environment. Because they reflect the environment around them, the best way to check whether a career is right for them is by looking at their health and energy levels. Many Reflectors are CEOs, run HR departments, work in start-ups, or are spiritual guides. Every Reflector's work life is going to look different. Ultimately, it is important that they get to provide feedback for how things are going and can go where the day leads them, all while taking breaks to rest when they need to. If they do not like their working situation, the best thing they can do is to start leaning in to their daily practice and surround themselves with communities and environments that feel supportive. This will naturally lead to them being invited to new opportunities and then using their Lunar Authority to make any big shifts.

Physical Body and Sleep

Alone time and time in nature are beneficial for a Reflector's physical body. They may feel that they have the energy to keep going all the time if they've been reflecting the energy levels of people around them, but this can lead to burnout if they are not prioritizing plenty of rest and sleep in their day-to-day life. Going to bed before they are very tired and having an hour to clear out and wind down before trying to sleep is ideal, and they can also experiment with sleeping alone to see how they feel. Some Reflectors find this supportive and others don't, so we encourage seeing what feels best.

When it comes to diet, Reflectors digest not only their food but also the energy of the environment and people they are around. It is best for them to be conscious of eating in environments and with people who feel extremely healthy or to try their best to eat alone.

For Reflectors who have a menstrual cycle, observing the connection between their body and the lunar energy of the moon and its cycle can be empowering and insightful.

Children

One of the most important things you can do to support Reflector children is to make sure their room and home or school environment and people feel healthy to them. Making small changes so things feel more in alignment for them can go a long way. Give them a lot of alone time to recharge and remember not to rush them in making decisions. Reflector parents can support their child by starting each day anew and not pressuring their child to be consistent in any way.

Relationships

The most important thing for Reflectors in romantic relationships is that they feel seen for who they truly are and not for who they are amplifying around them (particularly their romantic partner). This can sometimes be difficult to decipher, so having alone time to clear out can be the best way to know whether someone sees them for them or is just seeing and loving their own reflection. Reflectors will know whether a relationship is healthy for them if they consistently love who they are when they are around that person. Reflectors need to be given space to make their own decisions, especially if the tendency is for their partner to make the majority of decisions for them as a couple.

Reflector Not-Self Theme Quiz

Select the answer that best describes your current feelings. **Keep track of how many As, Bs, and Cs you select.**

My relationship to my family and other close supportive relationships:

A   It feels hard for me to be my true self with my family. I don't feel that they really understand me or include me in the way I crave to be included. They always want me to be less sensitive and more consistent with my interests.

B   The more I honor my sensitivity and empathy, the more accepting I am of myself. I notice that as I start to accept myself, my family is starting to as well.

C   I love that I am such a special and rare lunar being. I am completely falling in love with how my energy works and am using my empathy to connect with and understand my family and close friends even more. They embrace me and love my presence.

My relationship to my career/life purpose:

A   I have kind of given up thinking my career should be better. For the most part, no one truly loves their job;

that's just the way the world is. When I am at my workplace, I feel pretty off and can't wait to get home.

B   There are aspects of my current career that I feel really into. At certain moments I genuinely feel delighted to be there, experiencing it all and shining my wisdom. However, there are also parts of my career in which I feel like I'm playing a role and not getting to be my full self.

C   I love what I do. Every new day brings excitement and new energy. I feel really good in my work environment and love the energy of the people I'm around each day.

My relationship to my energy levels and physical well-being:

A   My digestion, sleep, and energy have been a bit off lately, but I try not to pay attention to that. If I stay busy, it doesn't bother me too much.

B   I'm starting to embrace that I am a truly sensitive person. I'm starting to make some more space for alone time and am paying attention to the

84

way my body communicates with me. However, I do notice that sometimes I try to hold on to the energy I feel from others when I'm alone instead of slowing down a bit.

C I love sharing in, riding out, and amplifying the energy of people around me, but I also really enjoy my alone time, when I can slow down, clear out, and tune in to nature. Overall, my health, sleep, and digestion are feeling really good.

My relationship to my romantic partner(s):

A Sometimes I feel like my partner really knows who they are and what they are doing in life, whereas I feel a bit lost, overwhelmed, and confused. Because of this, I like to let them take the lead in our major life choices.

B The more focused I am on observing the depths of all I pick up throughout each day of the lunar cycle, the more I am starting to trust in my own discernment. Even though I enjoy my partner's energy, I am starting to tell the difference between who I am versus who I am when I am reflecting them.

C I love who I am when I'm around my partner. They are healthy and authentic, and I love getting to share our life together. I enjoy creating my own space within our relationship too, and I feel like my partner really understands me. They hold space for me to take the time I need to come to my truth, and they want to hear my reflections on our life together.

My relationship with myself:

A I struggle with feeling like I don't know who I am or how to find myself. I can at times feel overwhelmed by being so sensitive and wish I could just find my thing already.

B I have been actively tuning in to feeling my connection with the lunar cycle more. I'm starting to see how deeply I can connect with others and how much wisdom I have to share. I am beginning to build my trust in the power of my design, but at times I still feel myself wanting to cling to things or try to get a grip on where my path is headed.

C I can genuinely say that I love myself and trust that I am always divinely guided and supported on my path. I feel safe and confident in my ability to flow through life without needing to cling to things.

MOSTLY AS: LIVING IN YOUR NOT-SELF

If you answered mostly As, you may be living in your not-self more often than not. You may be feeling disappointed and unclear about who you are quite frequently. This may be because you have been trying to identify with the things you have empathetically experienced instead of letting yourself shape-shift and flow.

Remember that the more you start observing who you become each day in a nonattached way, the more life will support you in bringing you all the people and places that are truly meant for you. You are experiencing such a special journey in this lifetime as a Reflector, so be kind, gentle, and nourishing to yourself.

MOSTLY BS: GROWING IN THE RIGHT DIRECTION

If you answered mostly Bs, you are finding your flow around living in personal alignment. There may be moments where you still feel disappointment, and that's okay! It's all about having awareness of when that not-self shows up and letting it prompt you back to clearing out your energy and observing your daily shifts.

You are beginning to prove to yourself that the more you focus on living life in your own unique, flowing way, the more you naturally find yourself in circumstances that feel good, where you feel connected and included to share your wisdom.

MOSTLY CS: FULL OF WISDOM AND WONDER

If you answered mostly Cs, you are mostly living in the realm of personal alignment! For the most part, you are experiencing life as a balanced, flowing, healthy Reflector who is able to be a true meter of authenticity and alignment.

Remember that as you develop patience in your connection to your unique lunar path, you open yourself up to being everything this world has to offer and being free from human identification. You are limitless, expansive, and always guided and held by life. What a beautiful and special role you have come here to play in this lifetime.

TIPS AND RECOMMENDATIONS FOR LIVING YOUR DESIGN

Tips

- **JOURNAL DAILY,** answering the question "Who am I today?"
- **CULTIVATE A DAILY RITUAL** for clearing your aura.
- **PRACTICE NONATTACHMENT** in every new circumstance or situation.
- **CREATE A "ZEN DEN" IN YOUR HOUSE** that is completely your own.
- **EAT AT LEAST ONE MEAL A DAY COMPLETELY ALONE** and outside in nature, if possible.

Supportive Crystals

- **APOPHYLLITE** for increasing awareness
- **HOWLITE** for patience
- **BLACK TOURMALINE** for cleansing your energetic field
- **KYANITE** for discernment
- **SELENITE** for resetting your energy

Essential Oils

- CLARY SAGE
- FRANKINCENSE
- MYRRH
- MELISSA

Meditations

- **DO A CORD-CUTTING MEDITATION.** Breathe deeply as you scan your aura. Picture an invisible light tool in your hand. It could look like a pair of sparkling scissors, a radiant pointed crystal, or a beautiful glowing blade. Move your hands around your body as you envision this light tool cutting away any strings of energetic attachment that are coming off of your aura. Repeat until all of the invisible strings have been completely detached.

- **GO TO OUR WEBSITE, DAYLUNALIFE.COM/FREE-HD-TOOLS,** to download our Chakra Clearing guided meditation. Follow along in a seated position.

- **ON THE NEW MOON, CREATE A CRYSTAL GRID** to amplify your intention. Grab five or more small crystals and find a space on a table. Place the first crystal down while stating what you would like to experience in this next lunar cycle. Use this first crystal as a center point and place the other crystals around it, creating a symmetrical mandala.

- **ON THE FULL MOON, STEP OUTSIDE IN THE MOONLIGHT** with your bare feet on the ground. As you stand there, set an intention for what you want to release in the next lunar cycle. Once you have clearly defined your intention, send the energy of what you want to shed down through your feet, discharging it into the Earth.

DECONDITIONING JOURNAL PROMPTS

- **What (people, job, personal attributes, etc.) am I currently identifying with?**

- **What comes up for me when I think about waiting** a month to make big decisions? Do I have any resistance or judgment there?

- **What decisions have I made when I felt rushed to decide?** How did that turn out for me? Do I feel authentically honored in where that decision led me?

- **What decisions have I made when I had a long time to consider?** How did that turn out for me? Do I feel authentically honored in where that decision led me?

- **Whom in my life have I felt the most alive around?**

- **In what environments have I felt the healthiest** and most in alignment?

- **How does my current living situation feel?**

- **How is my health and physical body right now?** Am I having any health issues?

- **Have I ever felt disconnected from nature?** What are ways that I can actively connect with nature (or the moon cycles) to support myself more?

- **How much alone time do I have?** Do I have resistance to spending time alone? If so, why might that be?

- **Are there any places in my life where I feel invisible?** If so, why? How can I cultivate time and rituals in which I can see myself more?

CHAPTER 4
The Eight Authorities

EVERY TIME WE MAKE AN IMPORTANT DECISION, we change the direction of our life to some degree. This is why many of us struggle with making decisions. We fear making the wrong choice and feel we must seek the guidance of others. When we lose trust in our own authentic truth from within, we give our authority away and begin to live from a place of insecurity, fear of the future, or regret for the past.

For thousands of years, our society as a whole has been living in a mental/ masculine paradigm. Humanity's main concern has been to survive: to have food, have shelter, ward off disease, and keep our children alive. Society has been focused on developing modern science, Western medicine, technology, and social and economic structures with the goal of making us stronger and more able to survive. With this mind-set at the forefront of our conditioning, we are taught that our own feelings and intuition have little value when it comes to creating our own life. We are programmed to take into consideration what the experts recommend and to weigh every important decision with our mind—to make the most reasonable, socially acceptable, practical, strategic, and justifiable choices. This mentally focused way of navigating life served the world when we were developing systems to survive and keep safe. However, the world is now rapidly changing and humanity is evolving into a new paradigm, a new way of being. Making decisions with our mind no longer serves us as individuals. Instead, it leads us to anxiety, fear, and self-doubt.

As a collective, we are moving into higher planes of consciousness and waking up to the truth that we are intrinsically connected to the flow of all life. We are each powerful, purposeful, unique beings who can feel what is right for ourselves.

This is where your Authority comes in. Your Authority is the decision-making process that helps you make important life decisions from a place of authentic alignment.

Understanding your Authority offers incredible insight on how to consistently feel your truth. This insight is by far one of the most life-changing aspects of Human Design. When we make decisions with our Authority, step by step, we begin creating a life that is correct for us. Our path begins to shape itself into the highest potential of what we came here to be and do. We feel a deep sense of sovereignty and empowerment. We learn to release self-doubt and be confident in our ability to navigate life.

Each one of the eight Authorities comes directly from a source in the body. For some, this Authority resides in a specific chakra center. For others, Authority arises from unique energies both within and outside of the body. Look to your chart to see which Authority you have and then find the corresponding section in this chapter.

Emotional Authority

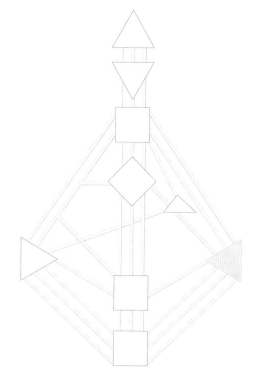

TRUTH COMES FROM:
The Solar Plexus Center

THE CENTER OF:
Emotions, Spiritual Awareness, Social Awareness

LEADING QUESTION: Does This Decision Make Me Happy?

DECISION TIME FRAME:
Wait at least Twenty-Four Hours, up to a Week.

Emotional Authority

Those who have Emotional Authority are designed to make important decisions by waiting until they come to an emotionally neutral place and feeling whether the opportunity is going to make them happy.

EMOTIONAL WAVES

If you have Emotional Authority, the first thing you need to understand is that your energy is designed to have an emotional wave. This means that while you have regular reactionary emotions to events occurring in your life, you also have a constant wave of emotional highs and lows that you experience at complete random. You can wake up on the right side of the bed for no reason, or you can wake up on the wrong side of the bed for no reason. Approximately half the population has Emotional Authority, which means approximately half of the world has an emotional wave and is experiencing emotions at random.

Although this may seem cumbersome or overwhelming, having an emotional wave is a gift that can help you learn emotional intelligence in this lifetime. It's a part of your design and thus a part of the unique life curriculum that your soul chose for you to experience.

Each emotion that arrives from your emotional wave is a teacher, a lesson giver, and an experience gifted to you to help you see your life from a new perspective. Each emotion you feel on your wave gives you a new level of understanding, a new level of depth. Over time, this depth helps you become more compassionate, resilient, and wise. With the wisdom you develop, you become a way-shower, sharing your emotional experiences and wisdom to help guide and empower others. In your highest expression, navigating your emotional wave is all about awareness and acceptance.

Your wave is meant to ebb and flow from high to low throughout the days and weeks. Without having awareness of this emotional wave, you can feel these emotional highs and lows and think, "What happened to cause this emotion?" You try to deem the emotion you feel as a repercussion of time you spent with a person or as punishment for a mistake you must have made. When you feel a low emotion, you try to identify with it by saying, "If I'm feeling depressed at this moment, then I myself must be a depressed person." When you try to identify the emotion you are experiencing as a defining part of yourself, then you actually end up holding on to the emotion and prolonging the amount of time you feel it, causing that emotion to stay with you for days, weeks, or even months.

Having awareness of where you are on your wave is key. If you had to guess, are you emotionally very high right now? Kind of high? Neutral? Kind of low? In a complete low/crash? Only by having this awareness of and familiarity with what the highs and lows of your wave feel like can you tell with certainty when you are neutral.

Make big life decisions only when you are emotionally neutral because your emotions color your truth.

It is imperative that you make big life decisions only when you are emotionally neutral because your emotions color your truth. When you are in an emotional high, you are more likely to feel positive about the decision at hand. Life feels good, you feel happy and in flow, and you don't realize you're in a high. When an opportunity is presented, you immediately think, "Yes, sign me up!" Then the next day comes and you instantly feel regret. "Why did I say yes?" you ask yourself. Because you were high on your wave.

The opposite is also true. When you are in a low, you can feel as though everything is a little harder. You feel a bit indifferent, melancholic, or gloomy. It can be subtle or obvious. Either way, it's this undertone that colors your overall experience throughout this time period. In this state, if an opportunity comes up, you can immediately think, "No way. It just doesn't sound good to me." The next day you can feel regret because now that you're neutral, the opportunity actually sounds good. You wish you had said yes.

The only time you can access your real truth is when you are emotionally neutral, and coming to that neutral place takes time. How much time? That depends. It could be a couple of hours from now or it could be a few days from now.

Acceptance is the other key ingredient to navigating life with an emotional wave. Because of our conditioning, many of us tend to judge our emotions and label them as good or bad. We are conditioned to see joy, happiness, and neutrality as "good" emotions—ones that we can be proud of, that make us healthy, and that are acceptable to share with others. We are conditioned to see depression, anxiety, and weariness as "bad" emotions—ones that we should be ashamed of, that make us unhealthy, and that we need to hide from other people. This type of labeling leads to a lack of acceptance within yourself and makes your emotional wave seem more difficult to experience.

You may notice that we use the terms *high* and *low* instead of *good* and *bad* when talking about the spectrum of emotions. Seeing your emotions this way brings acceptance. Your low emotions are beautiful gifts that move you to great depth. Feeling deep sadness empowers you to embody new levels of understanding, compassion for others, and gratitude for other parts of your life. When you have awareness of an emotion and allow yourself to fully feel it without labeling it as bad, without holding on to it and judging yourself as a person, you can navigate the wave as you are meant to.

Your emotions come in waves, in ebbs and flows. When you experience a low emotion, fear can pop up. "Will this last forever? Am I stuck in this perspective?" Taking comfort in the fact that this emotion will soon pass allows you to more easily accept it and learn the lesson it has for you.

TYPES OF EMOTIONAL WAVES

There are four types of emotional waves, and you may have one or several waves depending on your chart. If you have one of the channels listed below, you have that emotional wave. The numbers on either side of a channel are the numbers of the gates that join together to form that channel. The channel is named by using the gate numbers, so for example, Channel 59–6 is the channel from Gate 59 to Gate 6.

The Source of All Wave Mechanics: Channel 59–6

This is the most subtle of all the waves. It is a slow and steady rise and fall of emotional highs and lows. However, this wave intensifies when you are physically with other people, creating stronger, more intense emotions.

If this is your wave:

- YOUR ENERGY ATTRACTS INTIMACY and closeness with others.
- YOU WILL OFTEN FEEL HEIGHTENED AND DEEP EMOTIONS when you are with others.
- IT'S IMPORTANT TO SPEND TIME ALONE to become neutral and to make decisions when you are completely alone.

The Tribal Wave: Channel 19–49 and Channel 37–40

This wave is felt as swells of highs and lows building up pressure over time. The pressure releases by crashing into a low with an outburst of emotion, and it is then reset.

If you have this wave:

- YOUR WAVE IS CONNECTED TO WHETHER YOUR EMOTIONAL NEEDS are being met within your close relationships.
- YOU CRAVE CLOSENESS AND PHYSICAL TOUCH. Being able to connect in a physical way such as snuggling, hugging a friend, or petting an animal soothes you and makes the lows of your wave seem easier to manage.
- IT'S IMPORTANT FOR YOU TO VOICE YOUR NEEDS TO YOUR LOVED ONES. When you do this consistently, you'll notice that your wave crashes less often and feels less dramatic when it does crash.
- ACTIVITIES THAT GET YOU INTO YOUR BODY and please your senses help you feel more aware and empowered to navigate your wave.

The Individual Wave: Channel 22–12 and Channel 39–55

This wave is felt as mostly neutral emotions with spikes down to low emotions, back to mostly neutral, and then spikes up to high emotions.

If you have this wave:

- YOUR WAVE HAS AN ENERGY THAT IS DEEPLY INDIVIDUALIZED and creates a personal rhythm that is unaffected by outside influence.
- WHEN YOU ARE IN THE HIGH OF YOUR WAVE, your energy is pointing you toward having fun, socializing, and reaching out to your friends and family.
- WHEN YOU ARE IN THE LOW OF YOUR WAVE, your wave is pointing you toward taking some alone time.
- YOUR LOW/ALONE TIME CAN BE A GREAT TIME TO CREATE and express yourself through a healthy creative outlet.
- YOUR HIGHS AND LOWS CAN PASS VERY QUICKLY, but if you are around people when you go into a low, the low can be prolonged. Taking five minutes to be alone can bring you back to neutral faster.

The Collective/Abstract Wave: Channel 41–30 and Channel 36–35

This wave is the most dramatic of the emotional waves. It is felt as a buildup to strong highs and crashes into deep lows.

If you have this wave:

- YOU HAVE A STRONG ABILITY TO IMAGINE a desired life, romantic partner, or outcome.
- WHEN YOUR DESIRES ARE NOT MET, you can experience a difficult crashing wave that is disproportionate to the situation that is actually happening.
- UNMET EXPECTATIONS CAN ALSO CAUSE a crash in your wave.
- TO NAVIGATE YOUR WAVE WITH MORE EASE, focus on releasing all expectations and being open to any outcome that may arise from a new experience.

MAKING DECISIONS WITH EMOTIONAL AUTHORITY

Every time an important life decision presents itself, give yourself time to find your clarity. You are not someone who is designed to "follow your gut" or just "go with your first instinct." You need time to feel it out.

Your Authority originates from your solar plexus chakra. When making a decision, take time to ride out your emotional wave to ensure you are neutral. From this neutral place, envision yourself actually doing the thing. Feel inside the core of your belly where your solar plexus chakra is:

- If you feel a definitive and obvious happiness sensation, expansion, and joy, and a smile is coming to your face, then you know this option is in alignment for you.

- If you feel overtly that it makes you feel not happy, weighed down, contracted, a knot in your stomach, or less of yourself, then you know this option is not in alignment for you.

- If you don't feel anything at all or if you feel something okay or mediocre, then it's important to say "no for now" to that decision. We often say yes to things that feel mediocre and end up wasting our energy on things that are not right for us.

Now, when picturing yourself doing this thing, you may also feel fear. Without awareness, fear can feel a lot like a no—it can bring about that same contracted feeling in your core. However, fear usually has energy behind the contraction. Behind the knot in your stomach, you may feel a buzzing, electricity, excitement, or nervousness. This is different from the sensation felt from a no. Something that is wrong for you feels like contraction with no energy or exhaustion behind it. If you are not sure whether what you are feeling is a no or fear, give yourself more time and come back to it in a few days.

Ideally you will find yourself saying, "I don't know why, but this just feels like it's going to make me happy" or "I don't know why, but this just doesn't feel like it's going to make me happy." This means you are making a decision with your body instead of your mind. You are not designed to be certain about the pros and cons or whether it is right or wrong, but you are designed to be certain whether something will make you happy or not. You are led toward alignment only by saying yes to things that make you feel undeniable happiness when you think about them.

Note: This is only for important decisions. For small decisions, trust yourself and go with the flow in the moment or if you're a Generator or a Manifesting Generator, use your Sacral Responses.

Quick Step-by-Step Guide to Making Decisions with Emotional Authority

1 **When a decision is first presented to you,** give yourself at least twenty-four hours and up to a week to come to your clarity.

2 **Ask yourself where you are on your emotional wave.** If you are high or low, continue to wait.

3 **Keep checking in** until you feel that you are emotionally neutral.

4 **From this neutral place, imagine yourself** doing the thing you are deciding on.

5 **Bring your awareness into your body.** Feel what emotions are showing up in the core of your body. If you feel an undeniable happiness, then it is in alignment for you to say yes to this decision.

6 **If you feel unclear or that something is mediocre,** then your answer is "no for now." If you think it's fear but you're not exactly sure, give yourself more time. Ride your emotional wave until you come to a neutral place again and then start this process over.

7 **The ultimate question you are asking yourself is,** "Does this make me feel happy?" If the answer is yes, then you have found something in alignment for you.

MAIN CONDITIONING FOR EMOTIONAL AUTHORITY

- The idea that you have to answer immediately or you will seem like you don't know what you want
- The idea that you need to hide your emotions when you are in your low
- The feeling that you are indecisive
- The label of dramatic
- The fear that you have bipolar disorder or depression because of your emotional wave
- The idea that people don't want to hear about your emotional experiences
- Constantly doubting yourself because you're holding on to how you felt about something when you were in a low

TIPS AND RECOMMENDATIONS

Tips

- WHEN YOU FIND YOURSELF OVERANALYZING YOUR DECISIONS, picture a white light in the center of your mind dropping down into your body. See if you can feel what emotions are in your body.
- SEE THAT YOUR EMOTIONAL WAVE IS GUIDING YOU to wait until you're neutral so that you can find your truth and take action in alignment with divine timing.
- USE KEY PHRASES, such as "Let me sleep on it and get back to you" or "That sounds interesting; can I check my schedule and let you know?" When you take the time you need, people will perceive that as confidence.
- AVOID ARGUING OR TRYING TO FIND RESOLVE during a confrontation when you are in a deep low or crash on your wave. You cannot feel your truth at this

time and may say things that you don't actually mean.

- **PRACTICE TELLING YOUR FRIENDS AND FAMILY ABOUT** where you are on your wave. Say things such as, "It has nothing to do with you, I'm just on a low on my wave today" or "I just woke up on the wrong side of the bed today and need a little bit of space."

Rituals

- **TRACK YOUR EMOTIONAL WAVE.** In the morning, write down where you are on your wave. Do this again in the afternoon and evening. This allows you to see how your emotional wave ebbs and flows.
- **WHEN YOU ARE EXPERIENCING AN INTENSE EMOTION,** ask yourself, "What is this perspective teaching me?"
- **SAY ALOUD THE FOLLOWING MANTRA:** "My emotions don't define me. They are experiences. I accept all of my emotions, the highs and the lows. They are equally beautiful gifts."
- **CELEBRATE YOUR HIGHS** by turning on happy music and dancing or singing, doing something playful or fun with friends, or writing a gratitude list.
- **CELEBRATE YOUR LOWS** by turning on sad music, letting yourself feel all the feels, having a good old-fashioned cry, or writing a letter or poem that expresses what you are feeling.
- **WHEN YOU WANT TO CLEANSE AN EMOTION** from your being after you are done feeling it, put your bare feet on the earth and set the intention to release your emotion into the ground for Mother Earth to absorb and transmute it.

Supportive Crystals

- YELLOW CALCITE
- TIGER'S EYE
- PYRITE
- CITRINE
- RUTILATED QUARTZ
- AMAZONITE

Essential Oils

- GERMAN CHAMOMILE
- WILD ORANGE
- YLANG-YLANG
- BERGAMOT
- CEDARWOOD
- SANDALWOOD

Sacral Authority

TRUTH COMES FROM:
The Sacral Center

THE CENTER OF:
Life Force Energy,
Creativity, Sexuality

LEADING QUESTION:
Do I want this?

DECISION TIME FRAME:
Immediately.

Sacral Authority

Those who have Sacral Authority are designed to make important decisions by listening to their immediate gut reaction on whether the opportunity feels exciting and is something they want.

SACRAL RESPONSES

If you have Sacral Authority, your energy is designed to have a consistent mechanical, energetic response when something excites you. Every time a small or big decision is presented, you feel an instant gut reaction of interest, excitement, ignition, inspiration, and a draw toward something—or not. We call these sensations sacral responses. This response sensation only happens when you are physically presented with stimuli in some way. Perhaps you are standing in front of an object associated with the decision, you read an email about it, or you hear a conversation or question about it. It is not possible to receive a true sacral response to a concept in your mind. A sacral response fades after the moment has passed, so be present and attuned to your body's response and take note of what the response is.

You are designed to trust yourself and make important life decisions spontaneously.

You are designed to trust yourself and make important life decisions spontaneously. Your Authority originates from inside your gut, in the core of your body, and says, "I don't know why, but I just want this," or "I don't know why, but I just don't want this." Your truth only speaks to you in the moment a decision arises. It's important to honor that truth and not second-guess yourself. Everyone's body uses a slightly different language to communicate with them:

- **A yes may feel like a desire** that pulls you in, gets your creative juices flowing, and energizes and excites every cell in your body. You may even hear the sound "ooo" come out of your mouth.

- **A no may feel like slight exhaustion,** a contraction in your gut, or like you are being repelled. You may even hear the sound "bleh" come out of your mouth as if you're spitting out food that was disgusting.

- **If you have no response** or if you feel something resembling okay or mediocre, then it's important to say "no for now" to that decision.

Your truth only speaks to you in the present moment, and whatever message it conveys can change from day to day. Something that is a "no for now" today may not be a no forever. If someone proposes the same opportunity the next day, you might be surprised to sense that in this new moment, your body is telling you, "Yes, this feels right," and now you have your new truth. Trust what your body is telling you. You do not need to judge it, try to make sense of it, or fear it will change in the future. If you listen to what it says in the now and take action accordingly, it will lead you toward alignment and the right place at the right time.

Quick Step-by-Step Guide to Making Decisions with Sacral Authority
1   **When a decision is first presented to you,** immediately bring your awareness to the gut feeling in the core of your body.

2 **The first reaction you feel in your body** is your truth. Do you feel excited? Do you *want* it?

3 **If you have a completely clear answer, great!** You have your truth. Now it's time to take action. There is no need to second-guess yourself or ask yourself why.

4 **If you do not get an immediate clear answer,** your answer is "no for now."

5 **If you feel contracted in your gut,** but there is energy behind it, this could just be fear. Allow the decision to be presented again and trust your excitement.

6 **In the end, the question** you are asking yourself is, "Do I want this?" If the answer is yes, you have found something in alignment for you.

MAIN CONDITIONING FOR SACRAL AUTHORITY

- The idea that it is irresponsible to not take a long time to consider your decisions
- Being afraid to trust yourself
- Fear of the future or that things won't work out
- The feeling that you have to be consistent or you will be seen as flaky
- The idea that your desires are not practical

TIPS AND RECOMMENDATIONS

Tips

- WHEN YOU FIND YOURSELF OVERANALYZING YOUR DECISIONS, picture a white light in the center of your mind dropping down into your body. See whether you can feel what your body's wisdom is telling you in your gut.
- IF YOU ARE HAVING TROUBLE WITH BEING DECISIVE, make sure that you are only presenting yourself with one decision at a time. Instead of thinking about ten different options at once, work through the various options one at a time.
- BEFORE GOING INTO A CONVERSATION in which you know you will be making deci sions, check in with your five physical senses to help ground you in your body.

103

- **AVOID ASKING YOURSELF WHETHER YOU ARE SURE.** This question is toxic for you and immediately brings you into your mind and out of your body.

Rituals

- **IN THE MORNING, DO A GROUNDING EXERCISE** (e.g., yoga, intentional breathing, tapping, dancing, or chanting mantras).
- **ALLOW YOURSELF TO MAKE PRIMAL REACTIONS TO FOOD.** Chanting, singing, and speaking aloud every day opens your throat chakra and helps you release your truth in the form of sacral sounds.
- **ADOPT THE PHRASE** "It's either a hell yes or a hell no for me."
- **SAY ALOUD THE MANTRA** "I trust myself" three times to help you embody self-trust.
- **USE YOUR CREATIVE ENERGY TO BUILD OR CREATE** something to help get the energy flowing openly in your sacral chakra.

Supportive Crystals

- CARNELIAN
- AMBER
- SUNSTONE
- SMOKEY QUARTZ
- SODALITE
- CHRYSOPRASE

Essential Oils

- ORANGE BLOSSOM
- CLOVE
- CARDAMOM
- CLARY SAGE
- PATCHOULI

Splenic Authority

TRUTH COMES FROM:
The Splenic Center

THE CENTER OF: Instincts,
Physical Safety, Intuition

LEADING QUESTION:
Does This Decision Feel Right?

DECISION TIME FRAME:
Immediately.

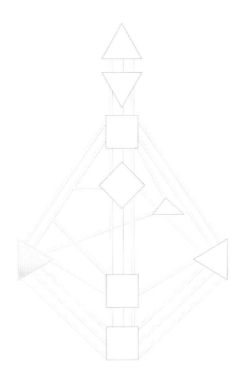

Splenic Authority

Those who have Splenic Authority are designed to make important decisions by listening to their immediate instinct about whether an opportunity feels right.

SPLENIC INTUITION

If you have Splenic Authority, your energy is designed to have consistently accurate instinctual feelings or intuition. Every time a small or big decision is presented to you, you feel an instant subtle sensation of response inside your body. This feeling is called splenic intuition. This intuition can be very quiet if you haven't been paying attention to it for most of your life. However, once you start using your awareness to intentionally listen to it, it will become clearer and more obvious over time.

MAKING DECISIONS WITH SPLENIC AUTHORITY

You are designed to make important life decisions spontaneously. Your truth only speaks to you once, in the very moment a decision arises. If you miss the signal and are not clear on what your splenic intuition indicated, you must hold off on making the decision. Allow the stimulus to be presented again and then tune in at that new moment to hear your body's response.

Your Authority originates from the core of your body and says, "I don't know why, but this just feels right" or "I don't know why, but this just feels wrong." Everyone with this Authority will describe the way they sense this information a little bit differently. Some people describe the feeling of their intuition as a quiet whispering voice. Others describe it as a lightness or expansion in their body or a heaviness or contraction in their body. Others say that something just smells right or smells off to them. Tune in and perceive how your body's intuition communicates to you.

As you tune in to your body, if you don't feel anything at all or if you feel something resembling okay or mediocre, then it's important to say "no for now" to that decision. Your truth only speaks to you in the present moment, and whatever message it conveys can change from day to day. Something that is a "no for now" may not be a no forever. If someone proposes the same opportunity the next day, you might be surprised to sense that in this new moment, your body is telling you, "Yes, this feels right," and now you have your new truth. Trust what your body is telling you. You do not need to judge it, try to make sense of it, or fear it will change in the future. If you listen to what it says in the now and take action accordingly, it will lead you toward alignment.

Splenic Authority comes from the splenic center, which is the energetic processing center in your body that creates primal instincts about your physical safety. This is also the place in the body where fear comes from. A healthy expression of fear alerts us when there might be danger. Your instincts guide you toward what you can do to keep yourself safe in that moment. When you have a lack of trust in your instincts and have avoided listening to them, you may notice that you often feel a sense of fear or anxiety. This is the lowest vibration of splenic intuition.

Building trust in your intuition is a life-changing journey for anyone with Splenic Authority. By experimenting with listening to your truth and following it, you can see how accurately your instincts guide you and start genuinely trusting yourself even more. Having this deep trust is the most important thing you can cultivate within yourself. It will alleviate any overindulged fears and anxiety you may be holding on to. You do not need to doubt your immediate instincts. You do not need time to decide. You do not need to rationalize why you know something is right for you. You just *know*. That is your truth. The more you can trust it, the more easily you will be able to navigate your life from one decision to the next in beautifully authentic alignment.

QUICK STEP-BY-STEP GUIDE TO
MAKING DECISIONS WITH SPLENIC AUTHORITY

1 **When a decision is first presented to you,** immediately bring your awareness to the core of your body.

2 **The first instinct you feel in your body is your truth.** Does it feel right or wrong?

3 **If you have a completely clear answer,** then great! You have your truth. Now it's time to take action.

4 **If you do not get an immediate clear answer,** your answer is "no for now."

5 **The same decision may present itself again later** and your intuition may give you a different answer.

6 **If you feel contraction in your body** but something about it still feels right, this could be fear. Allow the decision to be presented again and trust what feels right.

7 **In the end, the question you are asking yourself is,** "Does this feel right?" If the answer is yes, you have found something in alignment for you.

MAIN CONDITIONING FOR SPLENIC AUTHORITY

- The feeling that you have to be consistent or you will be seen as flaky
- Being afraid to trust yourself
- Fear of the future or that things won't work out
- Lack of self-worth or the feeling that you are not enough
- Playing it safe and not wanting to take risks
- Imposter syndrome when it comes to leading, teaching, or starting your own business

TIPS AND RECOMMENDATIONS

Tips

- **WHEN YOU FIND YOURSELF OVERANALYZING YOUR DECISIONS,** picture a white light in the center of your mind dropping down into your body. See whether you can feel what your body's wisdom is telling you.

- **BEFORE GOING INTO A CONVERSATION** in which you know you will be making decisions, check in with your five physical senses to help ground you in your body.

- **TAKE IMMEDIATE ACTION ON THE SMALL INSTINCTS** that come to you (e.g., to wash your hands, call a specific friend, or double-check something).

- **AVOID ASKING YOURSELF WHETHER YOU ARE SURE.** This question is toxic for you and immediately brings you into your mind and out of your body.

Rituals

- **IN THE MORNING, DO A GROUNDING EXERCISE** (e.g., yoga, intentional breathing, tapping, dancing, or chanting mantras).

- **USE ESSENTIAL OILS THROUGHOUT THE DAY** to connect with your sense of smell in a present and embodied way.

- **SAY ALOUD THE INTENTION,** "I am ready to deepen my connection to my intuition."

- **SAY ALOUD THE MANTRA** "I trust myself" three times to help you embody self-trust.

- **KEEP A JOURNAL** (or note file on your phone) to write down intuitive instincts you feel throughout the day.

- **GO OUTSIDE IN NATURE** to connect with the Earth on a regular basis.

Supportive Crystals

- BLACK TOURMALINE
- OBSIDIAN
- SPIRIT QUARTZ
- MOONSTONE
- SMOKY QUARTZ
- MERLINITE

Essential Oils

- CYPRESS
- BLACK PEPPER
- CLARY SAGE
- GRAPEFRUIT
- CLOVE

Ego-Projected Authority

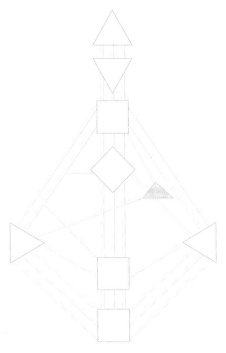

TRUTH COMES FROM:
The Ego/Heart Center

THE CENTER OF: Value,
Self-Worth, Motivation,
Willpower

LEADING QUESTION:
Does This Serve Me?

DECISION TIME FRAME:
Immediately or However Long
It Takes to Let Clarity Come

Ego-Projected Authority

Those who have Ego-Projected Authority are designed to make important decisions by asking themselves how the opportunity would benefit and serve them as an individual.

MAKING DECISIONS WITH EGO-PROJECTED AUTHORITY

If you have Ego Projected Authority, your energy is designed to have consistent motivation and drive. You are very connected to the material plane, and with this Authority you have significant openness in your design. That means you are deeply empathetic to the influence and energy of others. However, you have your own consistent way of seeing your self-worth, the way you value your time and energy, and your material desires. Every time a big decision is presented to you, you are designed to tune in to the energy coming from your ego/heart center.

To feel ego-projected energy within yourself, focus your awareness on the part of your chest where your physical heart is. Your truth is found by asking yourself, "How is this opportunity going to serve me? How is it going to benefit me? Will I be rewarded or compensated in a way that I want and desire? Is this something that

109

I truly desire? Is my heart fully in this?" You are looking to see whether you feel supported and pleased with how it's going to serve you.

This is one of the only Authorities for whom taking money into consideration when making an important life decision can be aligned. If you are deciding whether to accept a job offer, it is healthy to ask yourself whether the pay honors your worth and value.

Individuals with this Authority can have conditioning around this process. It may feel selfish or materialistic for you to consider these questions. You can be so empathetic that you get lost in other people's energy, emotions, and needs. However, the most empowering thing you can do is focus on yourself and not worry about the needs of other people. Human Design uses the phrase *enlightened selfishness* to describe this. The highest truth is that when you do something that is going to serve and benefit you, it's going to serve and benefit those around you as well; you will be able to operate at your highest potential and give your unique medicine to the world in a sustainable way.

Your Authority originates from inside the core of your chest. It says, "I don't know why, but this just feels like it's going to serve me," or "I don't know why, but this just doesn't feel like it's going to serve me." This may be a physical sensation of expansion with desire and excitement, or it may be a physical sensation of heaviness, as if your chest is sinking or contracting. Of course, every individual's body speaks to them differently, so it's important to tune in and notice how your heart feels when making these decisions. If you don't feel anything at all or if you feel something resembling okay or mediocre, that is your body saying "no for now." Opportunities will come up that will kind of serve you but that make you feel like saying yes would be sacrificing what you really deserve. You can often fear that something better won't come along. It is important in these cases to turn the mediocre opportunity down. If you say yes, you will be using your energy in a way that is out of alignment for you. This can result in burnout and bitterness.

Quick Step-by-Step Guide to Making Decisions with Ego-Projected Authority

1 **When a decision is first presented to you,** immediately bring your awareness to the feeling in your chest.

2 **Ask yourself how the decision will serve you.** Does it pay you an amount that excites and motivates you? Will it bring you influence and expansion in a way that benefits you? Is your heart completely in it?

3 If you have a completely clear answer rather quickly, great! You have your truth. Now it's time to take action.

4 If you do not get an immediate clear answer, give yourself more time to deliberate.

5 After feeling or talking it out more, clarity will eventually come as either "Yes, this does serve me; I want it" or "It seems okay, but feels like I'd be sacrificing my true value, so I'm definitely saying no."

6 If you feel that fear is clouding your ability to feel your Authority, give yourself more time and deliberate more.

7 In the end, the question you are asking yourself is, "Does this benefit me?" If the answer is yes, you have found something in alignment for you.

MAIN CONDITIONING FOR EGO-PROJECTED AUTHORITY

- Fear of being selfish
- The constant feeling of responsibility for taking care of others
- Fear of seeming overly materialistic
- The idea that having wealth and helping people can't go together
- The idea that the only way to be of service is to sacrifice yourself
- The feeling that you need to factor others' opinions into your decisions

TIPS AND RECOMMENDATIONS

Tips

- ONCE YOU HAVE ACQUIRED INFORMATION about the benefits of a choice, allow yourself to release them and focus your awareness on your body, specifically on your chest and heart space.
- IF YOU FIND YOURSELF GETTING STUCK and overanalyzing your decisions, picture a white light in the center of your mind dropping down into your chest. Tune in to what you feel in your heart.
- FEELING EXPANSION IN YOUR CHEST often indicates a yes, whereas a small contraction often indicates a no.

- **DON'T BE AFRAID TO ASK PEOPLE DIFFICULT QUESTIONS** to get the information you need to make an informed decision and feel out your truth.
- **CHECK IN TO SEE WHETHER YOU HAVE ANY LIMITING BELIEFS** around money or value and your own self-worth.

Rituals

- **DO A MEDITATION DURING WHICH** you release all limits and practical constraints and envision your ideal dream life. What does your dream life look like on the material plane? Without worrying about how you're going to get there, simply let your body vibrate at the frequency of this dream life.
- **FREEWRITE IN A JOURNAL** to consider the questions associated with your Authority. (See above.) Allow yourself to be completely honest, and don't worry about how it would sound if someone else read it.
- **PRACTICE CELEBRATING YOUR SELF-WORTH** by looking in the mirror and telling yourself what you deserve on the physical plane.
- **FIND A BREATHING EXERCISE** or workout routine that you love, but that is also challenging for you. Do this exercise every time you want to show yourself how strong your willpower can be when you are aligned with the task at hand.
- **SAY ALOUD THE FOLLOWING MANTRAS:** "I help the world the most when I only do things that serve, uplift, and sustain me." "I deserve the things that I desire. The things that I want are meant to be a part of my path."
- **SELECT PEOPLE YOU RESONATE WITH** and admire who have helped a lot of people and have also created a lot of wealth for themselves. Start reading about those people, familiarizing yourself with how their paths unfolded. Let their paths show you that your own dreams are possible.

Supportive Crystals

- MALACHITE
- GREEN JADE
- CITRINE
- CARNELIAN
- SMOKY QUARTZ
- AMAZONITE

Essential Oils

- BERGAMOT
- JASMINE
- GERANIUM
- LEMONGRASS
- GINGER

Ego-Manifested Authority

TRUTH COMES FROM:
The Ego/Heart Center

THE CENTER OF: Value,
Self-Worth, Motivation,
Willpower

LEADING QUESTION:
Does This Serve Me?

DECISION TIME FRAME:
Immediately or However Long
It Takes To Let Clarity Come

Ego-Manifested Authority

Those who have Ego-Manifested Authority are designed to make important decisions by asking themselves how the opportunity would benefit and serve them and then answering that question aloud in a completely unfiltered way to hear their truth.

MAKING DECISIONS WITH EGO-MANIFESTED AUTHORITY

Ego-Manifested Authority is very similar to Ego Projected Authority in that your energy is designed to have consistent motivation and drive. You are very connected to the material plane, and you have significant openness in your design. You are deeply empathetic to the influence and energy of others, but you have your own consistent way of seeing your self-worth, the way you value your time and energy, and your material desires. Every time a big decision is presented, immediately open your mouth and speak without trying to control what you say. Your voice will carry the consistent energy from your ego/heart center out through your throat so you can hear your truth coming straight from your heart.

Your truth is found by asking yourself, "How is this opportunity going to serve me? How is it going to benefit me? Will I be rewarded or compensated in a way that I want? Is this something that I truly desire? Is my heart fully in this?" You can talk aloud to yourself, to the universe, or to a trusted friend. However, you must do so in a completely candid, open, vulnerable, and authentic manner. If you feel unsafe speaking your truth or you subconsciously feel that you might be judged for what comes out, you can end up filtering yourself and you will not receive clarity from what you end up saying. You are trying to hear yourself say that you feel supported and pleased with how this decision is going to serve you.

This is one of the only Authorities for whom taking money into consideration when making an important life decision can be aligned. If you are deciding whether to accept a job offer, ask yourself whether the pay honors your worth and value. Then, without thinking, answer aloud.

You may have conditioning around this process; it may feel selfish or materialistic for you to consider these questions. You can be so empathetic that you get lost in other people's energy, emotions, and needs. But the most empowering thing you can do is focus on yourself and not worry about the needs of other people. Human Design uses the phrase *enlightened selfishness* to describe this. The highest truth is that when you do something that is going to serve and benefit you, it's going to serve and benefit those around you as well; you can operate at your highest potential and give your unique medicine to the world in a sustainable way.

When a decision is right for you, you will be confident, you won't have any hesitation or doubts, and the tone of your voice will reveal excitement, desire, or enthusiasm. You might say something like, "This is going to bring me closer to my goals or dream life." When something is not in alignment for you, your tone may be disappointed or indifferent, and you may even use negative words. You will have the physical sensation of heaviness, as if your chest is sinking or contracting. Phrases such as "I feel bad" or "I guess I could" are a sure sign that the option is not in alignment for you. If you don't feel anything at all or if you feel something resembling okay or mediocre, that is your body saying "no for now." Opportunities that kind of serve you will come up. You may feel like saying yes would be sacrificing what you really want and deserve, but you're afraid that something better won't come along. Turn that mediocre option down. If you say yes to it, you will be using your energy in a way that is out of alignment for you. This can result in feeling angry and burned out.

Quick Step-by-Step Guide to Making Decisions with Ego-Manifested Authority

1 **When a decision is first presented to you,** don't take time to think; just open your mouth and say your response out loud, completely unfiltered.

2 **Ask yourself how the decision would serve you.** Does it pay you an amount that excites and motivates you? Will it bring you influence and expansion in a way that benefits you? Is your heart completely in?

3 **Listen to what comes out of your mouth.** If you have a completely clear answer rather quickly, great! You have your truth. Now it's time to take action.

4 **If you do not get an immediate clear answer,** talk it out and give yourself time or let the question come up again naturally. Repeat this process until you hear your clarity through your voice as either "Yes, this does serve me; I want it" or "It seems okay, but feels like I'd be sacrificing my true value, so I'm definitely saying no."

5 **If you feel that fear or limiting beliefs** are clouding your ability to feel your Authority, have the conversation again until your voice feels truly unfiltered.

6 **In the end, the question to yourself is,** "Does this benefit me?" If you verbally answer yes, then you have found something in alignment for you.

MAIN CONDITIONING FOR EGO-MANIFESTED AUTHORITY

- Fear of sharing your vulnerable truth and overediting yourself
- Fear of offending people
- Fear of being selfish
- Constantly feeling responsible for taking care of others
- Fear of seeming overly materialistic
- The idea that having wealth and helping people can't go together
- The idea that the only way to be of service is to sacrifice yourself
- The feeling that you need to consider others' opinions in your decisions

TIPS AND RECOMMENDATIONS

Tips

- ONCE YOU HAVE ACQUIRED INFORMATION about the benefits of a choice, allow yourself to release it and simply start speaking aloud.
- IF YOU FIND YOURSELF GETTING STUCK and overanalyzing your decisions, picture a white light in the center of your mind dropping down into your chest. Tune in to what you feel in your physical chest and picture your heart energy coming up in a stream that pours out of your voice.
- FEELING EXPANSION IN YOUR CHEST often indicates a yes for you, whereas feeling a small contraction often indicates a no.
- DON'T BE AFRAID TO ASK PEOPLE DIFFICULT QUESTIONS to find the information you need to make an informed decision and feel out your truth.
- CHECK IN TO SEE WHETHER YOU HAVE ANY LIMITING BELIEFS around money and your own self-worth.

Rituals

- DO A MEDITATION IN WHICH YOU RELEASE ALL LIMITS and practical constraints and envision your ideal dream life. What does your dream life look like on the material plane? Without worrying about how you're going to get there, simply let your body vibrate at the frequency of this dream life.
- FREEWRITE IN A JOURNAL to consider the questions associated with your Authority (see above). Allow yourself to be completely honest, and don't worry about how it would sound if someone else read it.
- PRACTICE CELEBRATING YOUR SELF-WORTH by looking in the mirror and telling yourself what you deserve on the physical plane.
- FIND A BREATHING EXERCISE or workout routine that you love, but that is also challenging for you. Do this exercise every time you want to show yourself how strong your willpower can be when you are aligned with the task at hand.
- SAY ALOUD THE FOLLOWING MANTRAS: "I help the world the most when I only do things that serve, uplift, and sustain me." "I deserve the things that I desire. The things that I want are meant to be a part of my path." "It is safe for me to speak my truth. My truth is not going to offend people; it's neutral."
- SELECT PEOPLE YOU RESONATE WITH and admire who have helped a lot of people and have also created a lot of wealth for themselves. Start reading about those people, familiarizing yourself with how their paths unfolded. Let their paths show you that your own dreams are possible.

Supportive Crystals

- MALACHITE
- LAPIS LAZULI
- CITRINE
- CARNELIAN
- LARIMAR
- AMAZONITE

Essential Oils

- LEMONGRASS
- PEPPERMINT
- SANDALWOOD
- GINGER
- GERANIUM

Self-Projected/ G Center Authority

TRUTH COMES FROM: The G Center

THE CENTER OF: Love, Purpose, Life Direction

LEADING QUESTION: Does This Decision Bring Me Closer To My Life's Direction?

DECISION TIME FRAME: Immediately or However Long It Takes To Let Clarity Come Through Speaking Aloud

Self-Projected/G Center Authority

Those who have Self-Projected/ G Center Authority are designed to make important decisions by candidly speaking out loud and listening to whatever comes out to hear their truth.

MAKING DECISIONS WITH SELF-PROJECTED/G CENTER AUTHORITY

If you have Self-Projected Authority, your energy is designed to use your voice to say aloud the thoughts that have been swirling around in your mind. You may try to silently deliberate for days and never feel clarity on what is right for you. However, once you open your mouth and let yourself talk freely about the options presented to you, your inconsistent and unintelligible strands of ideas will suddenly transform into a linear and revealing statement.

If you have this Authority, you are gifted at seeing the direction others should take and naturally feel inclined to give others your insight and guidance. However, when it comes to seeing your own path or your own sense of self, you can feel unclear. This is not because you don't have a clear sense of direction. On the contrary, you have an incredibly consistent unique identity and purpose in this lifetime, which others plainly recognize in you. It's just that, for you to know yourself, you must speak aloud. You don't realize how you really feel about something until the energy from your G center is released from your throat.

It's helpful for you to cultivate relationships with loyal, reliable people who accurately see and accept you. Whenever you need to make a decision or find clarity, have a conversation with one of these confidants. By speaking with them, you are not asking for their opinion or advice, but rather using them as a supportive witness to your own personal process. Ask them to share the level of excitement or disinterest they hear in your voice. While you are listening to yourself speak, pay attention to your tone; excitement, passion, confidence, and a heartfelt drawl are all signs of something being right for you.

After speaking for as long as you naturally feel inclined to and listening to what you say, you will at some point reach an obvious conclusion. You will feel in your body (specifically in your chest) that this thing is undeniably right for you and is leading you down the right path.

Quick Step-by-Step Guide to Making Decisions with Self-Projected Authority

1 **When making a decision or to find clarity,** open your mouth and start voicing whatever comes to you about the situation at hand. Try not to edit yourself, but instead allow yourself to be honest and unattached to whatever comes out for you. This can be speaking to yourself, to the universe, or to a loving and trusted friend. You may feel awkward at first, but once you begin warming up your voice and opening your throat chakra, you will start to feel the energy flowing within your speech.

2 **Ask yourself one of the following questions:** "Does this bring me closer to my purpose in life?" "Does this bring me closer to where I want to be?" "Is this in alignment with my passions/mission/beliefs?"

3 **Listen to the truth that is being revealed with your words.** If you'd like, ask a friend to help by listening too. The statements that just pop out of your mouth may surprise you. Listen for not only the content of what you are saying but also the tone and inflection.

4 **Continue talking and listening** until you have absolute clarity that you can feel in your chest and body, as if you are being pulled toward or away from this decision.

5 **If you feel that fear is clouding your ability to feel** your Authority, keep talking. Talk about the fears you may have around this decision.

6 **In the end, the question you are asking yourself is,** "Does this bring me closer to my life direction?" If the answer is yes, you have found something in alignment for you.

MAIN CONDITIONING FOR SELF-PROJECTED AUTHORITY

- The feeling that you speak too much or take up too much space
- Not wanting to be the center of attention
- The feeling that you cannot speak aloud or a fear around public speaking
- Feeling as if you are needy or dependent on others
- Not knowing who you are or what your direction is
- Feeling lost

TIPS AND RECOMMENDATIONS

Tips

- PHRASES SUCH AS "I FEEL LIKE I SHOULD," "I have to," "I guess I could," or "I feel bad for them" are all signposts that the option is not right for you.
- JOURNAL AND ALLOW YOURSELF TO FREEWRITE, and then read aloud what you wrote.

- **WARM UP YOUR VOICE BY TALKING ABOUT SOMETHING** that feels effortless (such as what you ate for breakfast or a good movie you watched recently).
- **WHEN YOU ARE CREATING CONTENT FOR WORK,** turn on a tape recorder and allow yourself to speak about your ideas.

Rituals

- **IN THE MORNING,** say aloud three intentions.
- **IN THE EVENING,** say aloud three things you are grateful for.
- **REGULARLY TALK ALOUD TO YOURSELF.** Practice saying daily affirmations, singing chants, reading books aloud, or singing in the shower to loosen up your throat chakra.
- **INSTEAD OF MEDITATING IN SILENCE,** try speaking aloud to the universe.
- **TO HELP YOU HONE YOUR LIFE DIRECTION,** freewrite on the following journal prompts: "I passionately believe that . . . ," "When I picture my ideal life, I am . . . ," and "The thing I care about most right now is . . ."
- **CULTIVATE MANTRAS TO SAY OUT LOUD** to yourself when you are feeling ungrounded.

Supportive Crystals

- GARNIERITE
- LEMURIAN SEED QUARTZ
- ROSE QUARTZ
- PREHNITE
- AMAZONITE

Essential Oils

- CLARY SAGE
- MAGNOLIA
- GREEN MANDARIN
- GERANIUM
- LAVENDER

Mental/Environmental Authority

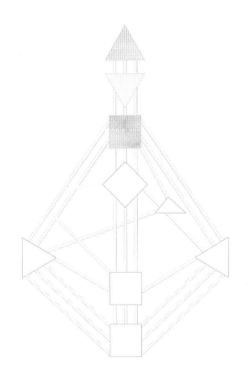

TRUTH COMES FROM:
The Entire Body

LEADING QUESTION:
Does This Decision Feel Right?

DECISION TIME FRAME:
After You Have Been Able to Process and Find Clarity.

Mental/Environmental Authority

You will only have this Authority if you are a Projector. Your chart may say "Inner Authority: None."

Those who have Mental/Environmental Authority are designed to make important decisions by giving themselves time to mentally consider and spending time in different environments until they feel clarity in their body.

MAKING DECISIONS WITH MENTAL/ENVIRONMENTAL AUTHORITY

If you have Mental/Environmental Authority, all of the centers in your body below your throat are undefined. This means that you have an ability for extreme empathy and can feel the world around you very deeply. All of that openness gives you the potential for wisdom, but it also can be overwhelming to take in other people's energy, fears, and emotions. If you have this Authority, the biggest consistent part of your energy is your brilliant mind. This is why Human Design calls you a Mental Projector.

Human Design teaches that we are designed to make important life decisions with our body and not our mind. So if you have Mental Authority, you may be thinking by now, "Wait, what? Why is my Authority called Mental Authority?" Your Authority is the one partial exception to this rule. Your energy is designed to use your mind to look at the details and facts of a decision. However, there are three steps in your process that you can use to find clarity:

1 **Engage in mental deliberation.** Every time a big decision is presented to you, allow yourself to look at all the details, facts, data, finances, and pros and cons lists. Once you fully consider everything on the drawing board and you feel satisfied with that part of the process, then it's time to completely set that aside.

2 **Physically go to environments that you love.** Go spend time in a places you feel really good in: your backyard, a park, a coffee shop, a lookout, the library, or the like. While in this space, you will feel new energies coming into your body and shedding new light on the decision.

3 **Talk about the decision with a trusted friend.** Bounce ideas off of a friend. Bonus points if you do this in one of your favorite environments.

Repeat these steps as needed, writing a new list, going to a new environment, and then maybe another one, and then maybe calling a close friend until you have a feeling of complete and absolute clarity.

Although the first step of this decision-making process is using your mind to weigh out the information associated with the decision, you are not actually designed to make the final decision with your mind. That part of the process is simply to satiate your mind and put it at ease. When you go to a new environment, a feeling of clarity in the core of your body is what you are actually looking for. It feels expansive and light, like an epiphany felt throughout your body. "Aha! I got it. I just know what I am going to do. This just feels right." Everyone with this Authority will describe what this sense of knowing feels like in their body a little bit differently. Tune in and perceive how your body communicates with you.

When working your way through this process, if you don't feel anything at all (neither right nor wrong) or if you feel something resembling okay or mediocre, then it's important to say "no for now" to that decision. As a Mental Projector, you don't have a large surplus or consistent amount of energy. When you say yes to things that you are not clear on, you end up wasting your precious energy resources on something that is not aligned for you. One of the most powerful ways to use your energy is to really focus on saying no to anything that is not a 100 percent "Yes, this just feels right."

Quick Step-by-Step Guide to Making Decisions with Mental/Environmental Authority

1 **When a decision is first presented to you,** gather all the data and mentally sort through it.

2 **When you have looked at everything,** get up and physically change environments.

3 **In a new environment that feels good to you,** think about the decision. If you feel a sense of complete clarity arrive in your body, great! You have your truth. Now it's time to take action.

4 **If you do not get a clear answer,** go to a different environment. You can also try calling a trusted friend and bouncing your ideas off of them. Until clarity arrives, continuing working with your three tools:

 a Mentally analyzing
 b Going to environments you love
 c Talking it out

5 **If you feel that fear is clouding your ability** to feel your Authority, give yourself more time to use your three tools.

6 **In the end, the question you are asking yourself is,** "Does this feel right?" If the answer is yes, you have found something in alignment for you.

MAIN CONDITIONING FOR MENTAL/ENVIRONMENTAL AUTHORITY

- The idea that you are indecisive
- The feeling that you need to hide your sensitivity
- Feeling constant pressure to overanaylze

- The idea that you need to work hard and climb the corporate ladder to find success
- Feeling the need to look to others to find answers
- Distrust in feelings that can't be rationalized
- Feeling disconnected from your body's wisdom

TIPS AND RECOMMENDATIONS

Tips

- **WHEN YOU GET STUCK IN THE ANALYZING PART** of your decision-making process and have trouble letting go of your mental pressure to figure things out, picture a white light in the center of your mind dropping down into your body. See whether you can feel what your body's wisdom is telling you.
- **LIMIT THE AMOUNT OF TIME YOU SPEND** in environments that feel wrong/off as much as possible. Trust that these places and the relationships you make there will be out of alignment for you.
- **CULTIVATE TECHNIQUES AROUND THE MENTAL ANALYSIS PART** of your process that feel fun for you—for example, write pros and cons lists, draw graphs, make spreadsheets, label with fun colors, or journal.
- **CULTIVATE TWO FAVORITE ENVIRONMENTS IN YOUR HOME** (e.g., looking out your front window, sitting in your bathtub, or sitting in your favorite nook). Then cultivate three favorite environments in your town and three that are an hour away from your home. Use these places often when you are trying to get a fresh perspective on things.

Rituals

- **IN THE MORNING, DO A GROUNDING EXERCISE** (e.g., yoga, intentional breathing, tapping, dancing, or chanting mantras).
- **SMUDGE WITH SAGE OR PALO SANTO** to clear unwanted energy from your aura or home.
- **SAY ALOUD THE INTENTION** "I am sorting this out to put my mind at ease and then I'm letting it go."
- **SAY ALOUD THE MANTRA** "I give myself as much time as I need for clarity to come" three times to help you embody patience in your process.
- **TO GIVE GRATITUDE AND BUILD YOUR CONNECTION** with a favorite place in

your home, put an offering there. This could be a crystal placed with this intention, burned incense, or a vase of flowers, for example.

- **GO OUTSIDE IN NATURE** to connect with the Earth on a regular basis.

Supportive Crystals

- AMETHYST
- LAPIS LAZULI
- BLACK TOURMALINE
- MOONSTONE
- PICTURE JASPER
- SODALITE

Essential Oils

- CYPRESS
- JUNIPER
- CLARY SAGE
- PEPPERMINT
- FRANKINCENSE

Lunar Authority

TRUTH COMES FROM: The Entire Body

LEADING QUESTION: Does This Decision Feel Right?

DECISION TIME FRAME: After an Entire Lunar Cycle

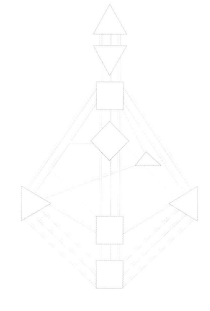

Lunar Authority

You will only have this Authority if you are a Reflector. Your chart may say "Inner Authority: None."

Those who have Lunar Authority are designed to make important decisions by waiting a 28 day lunar cycle and letting clarity come.

MAKING DECISIONS WITH LUNAR AUTHORITY

If you have Lunar Authority, then you are a part of the amazing 1 percenters: Reflectors! As a Reflector, your energy is deeply connected with and affected by the moon's energy. Every day, the moon's powerful energy shifts and moves into new gates in the Human Design chart, and this is experienced within your body as new parts of you being illuminated each day—new qualities popping up to be felt and experienced.

When making small decisions, you are designed to go with the flow, to do whatever feels right in the moment. However, when an important or big life decision presents itself, you are designed to give yourself at least twenty-eight days (one lunar cycle) to allow clarity to come to you.

As a Reflector, you have all nine of your centers undefined. This means that in all of these different energy centers, not only are you absorbing the moon's energy shifts but you are also constantly taking in the energy of all the people and environments you are in and around. It is tempting to make important decisions about your life quickly when you are with someone who has a spontaneous decision-making process. And although you are here to share in their energy that day, you are not here to make life decisions with the temporary influence of their energy. Doing so can cause you to slip out of personal alignment. This is why it is imperative that you give yourself a full twenty-eight days to process something before committing to it.

When a big life decision arises, check to see what phase of the moon we are currently in and wait for the next time the moon is in that phase. For example, if it is a new moon, give yourself until at least the next new moon for clarity to come. At the end of each day of the 28 day cycle, ask yourself, "Who was I today? How did I feel about this decision?" Fully honor and observe what you felt your answer was that day without needing to pressure yourself to call this your truth or attach yourself to what you experienced. Take note of what you experienced, fully witness it, and then let it go. The next day, do it again.

Eventually, your Authority will resonate a feeling from inside the core of your body that says, "I don't know why, but this just feels right" or "I don't know why, but this just feels wrong." Everyone with this Authority will describe the way they sense this information a little bit differently. You may feel lightness or expansion when it is a yes or a heaviness or contraction in your body when it is a no.

When working your way through this process, if you don't feel any clarity at all (neither right nor wrong) or if you feel something resembling okay or mediocre, then it's important to say "no for now" to that decision. If you are not exactly sure about what you feel, even if the lunar cycle you were waiting through has passed, then give yourself more time. As a non-energy being, your energy resources are precious and somewhat limited. Saying yes to things that you do not have absolute clarity on will leak your energy and lead to your committing to things that are not right for you.

Quick Step-by-Step Guide to Making Decisions with Lunar Authority

1 **When a decision is first presented to you,** check to see what phase the moon is in. Is it a full moon? A new moon? A waxing gibbous? Take note and give yourself 28 days—until the next time the moon is in that phase—to make the decision.

2 **Each day of the 28 days,** ask yourself, "Who was I today? How did I feel about this decision?" Fully witness and observe this without any pressure or judgment for it to be your final answer.

3 **If you feel absolute clarity** and a sense of knowing come into your entire being by the last day of the 28 day period, when the moon has returned to the position it was in when you started, great! You have your truth. Now it's time to take action.

4 **If you do not feel a clear answer,** then your answer is no for now. Give yourself another 28 day cycle to find clarity.

5 **Continue to check in each day** and ask what you felt yourself become that day and how that made you feel about your decision.

6 **If you feel that fear is clouding your ability** to feel your Authority, give yourself more time.

7 **In the end, the question you are asking yourself is,** "Does this feel right?" If the answer is yes, then you have found something in alignment for you.

MAIN CONDITIONING FOR LUNAR AUTHORITY

- THE FEELING THAT YOU HAVE TO RUSH YOURSELF or you will be seen as flaky or irresponsible
- BEING AFRAID TO TRUST YOURSELF
- BEING AFRAID THAT IF YOU TAKE YOUR TIME nothing will happen or that you will fall behind
- FEELING SCARED TO OBSERVE or admit the way your feelings about your decision change every day
- PLAYING IT SAFE by letting your partner or family members make decisions for you
- THE FEELING THAT YOU NEED TO HIDE your sensitivity to appear competent in navigating your life

TIPS AND RECOMMENDATIONS

Tips

- WHEN YOU FIND YOURSELF OVERANALYZING YOUR DECISIONS, picture a white light in the center of your mind dropping down into your body. See whether you can feel what your body's wisdom is telling you.
- CREATE A JOURNALING PRACTICE that you love and that is sustainable for you, whether that is as simple as writing a couple of words on a calendar or creating a thoroughly organized spreadsheet that you track your daily process in.
- GET A MOON CALENDAR so you can keep track of the lunar cycle easily.
- TALK ABOUT YOUR DECISION with a trusted family member or friend, not to get their opinion but to simply allow your ideas to bounce off of them and come back to you.
- BUY THE LUNAR TRANSIT TOOL on mybodygraph.com to see the exact way your design changes each day with the lunar cycles.

Rituals

- IN THE MORNING, DO A GROUNDING EXERCISE (e.g., yoga, intentional breathing, tapping, dancing, or chanting mantras).
- IF YOU HAVE A MENSTRUAL CYCLE, track it alongside the moon cycle.
- SPEND TIME IN THE MOONLIGHT.
- SAY ALOUD THE INTENTION "I am ready to honor my connection to the moon."

- **SAY ALOUD THE MANTRA** "I give myself as much time as I need for clarity to come" three times to help you embody self-trust.
- **ESTABLISH A RITUAL THAT HELPS YOU CLEANSE YOUR ENERGY** when you have been around a lot of people. This could be, for example, saging yourself, using palo santo, or taking a cleansing salt bath.
- **GO OUTSIDE IN NATURE** to connect with the Earth on a regular basis.

Supportive Crystals

- BLACK TOURMALINE
- BLUE LACE AGATE
- MOOKAITE
- MOONSTONE
- SELENITE
- PEARL

Essential Oils

- PATCHOULI
- YLANG-YLANG
- ROSEMARY
- CORIANDER
- FRANKINCENSE

CHAPTER 5

Combining Strategy & Authority

S TRATEGY AND AUTHORITY (S&A) ARE the most important teachings of Human Design. Together they create a reliable navigation system that empowers you to become your own expert in living your most authentic life. The more you lean into your S&A, the more you will naturally find personal alignment and the better you will live out your purpose. You actually do not need to understand anything further in your Human Design chart (gates, channels, Profile, etc.), even though it is wildly insightful and fascinating. If you understand and start using your S&A, everything else will fall into place in the highest expression naturally.

What Does Following S&A Look Like?

For Manifestors with Emotional Authority
- Using your voice to inform people (and the universe) about where you are, what you feel, what you envision, and the like.
- When a big decision comes, giving yourself plenty of time to come to neutral and then choosing what will make you happy.

For Manifestors with Splenic Authority
- Using your voice to inform people (and the universe) about where you are, what you feel, what you envision, and the like.
- When a big decision comes, immediately tuning in to your body's subtle intuition and then choosing what feels right to you.

For Manifestors with Ego-Manifested Authority
- Using your voice to inform people (and the universe) about where you are, what you feel, what you envision, and the like.
- When a big decision comes, immediately speaking, unfiltered, to hear your truth, and then choosing what will benefit you most.

For Generators with Emotional Authority
- Engaging with the things in your present environment that your body responds to with sacral energy, desire, and excitement.
- When a big decision comes, giving yourself plenty of time to come to neutral and then choosing what will make you happy.

For Generators with Sacral Authority
- Engaging with the things in your present environment that your body responds to with sacral energy, desire, and excitement.
- When a big decision comes, trusting your gut's enthusiasm in the present moment and then choosing what excites you.

For Manifesting Generators with Emotional Authority
- Engaging with the things in your present environment that your body responds to with sacral energy, desire, and excitement, and informing those around you along the way.
- When a big decision comes, giving yourself plenty of time to come to neutral and then choosing what will make you happy.

For Manifesting Generators with Sacral Authority
- Engaging with the things in your present environment that your body responds to with sacral energy, desire, and excitement, and informing those around you along the way.

- When a big decision comes, trusting your gut's enthusiasm in the present moment and then choosing what excites you.

For Projectors with Emotional Authority

- Focusing on yourself and waiting to be invited before sharing your advice, insight, or services with others.
- When a big decision comes, giving yourself plenty of time to come to neutral and then choosing what will make you happy.

For Projectors with Splenic Authority

- Focusing on yourself and waiting to be invited before sharing your advice, insight, or services with others.
- When a big decision comes, immediately tuning in to your body's subtle intuition and then choosing what feels right to you.

For Projectors with Ego-Projected Authority

- Focusing on yourself and waiting to be invited before sharing your advice, insight, or services with others.
- When a big decision comes, deliberating on how an option will serve you and then choosing what will benefit you most.

For Projectors with Self Projected/G Center Authority

- Focusing on yourself and waiting to be invited before sharing your advice, insight, or services with others.
- When a big decision comes, speaking aloud so you can hear your truth and then choosing what will bring you closer to your unique life direction.

For Projectors with Mental/Environmental Authority

- Focusing on yourself and waiting to be invited before sharing your advice, insight, or services with others.
- When a big decision comes, analyzing all the facts and figures and then spending time in your favorite environments until you feel absolute clarity in your body. Then choosing what feels right for you.

For Reflectors with Lunar Authority
- Reflecting each day on who you became that day and then choosing to let it go to return back to your own energy.
- When a big decision comes, giving yourself an entire 28 day lunar cycle to feel into your body until you have undeniable clarity. Then choosing what feels right for you.

CHAPTER 6

Deeper Dive: Centers

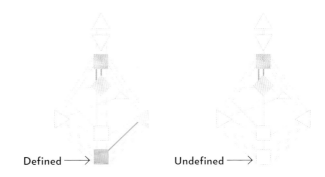

Defined ⟶   Undefined ⟶

WHEN YOU FIRST LOOK AT your Human Design chart, you will see a bodygraph with triangles, squares, and a diamond. The shapes are either white or colored in, and they represent the nine energy-processing centers of the body. The centers in your chart that are colored in are defined, and the centers that are white are undefined or open.

Think of all your energy centers as the areas in which you give or receive energy. In your defined centers, you consistently give out your own energetic frequency, influencing others. In your undefined/open centers, you empathetically take in and experience an amplified version of the energy that comes from the people around you who have those specific centers defined. The configuration of your activated gates determines which of your centers are defined and which are undefined. (To learn about gates, see chapter 8.)

The centers are broken down into five categories:

Manifestation Center

Throat

Pressure Centers

Head

Root

Awareness Centers

Ajna

Splenic

Solar plexus

Identity Center

G center

Motor (Energy) Centers

Root

Sacral

Solar plexus

Ego/heart

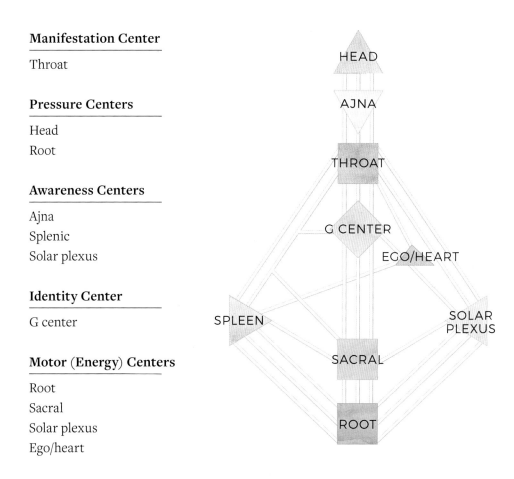

The centers show the areas in which you are meant to condition others and the areas in which you take in conditioning. When you are in personal alignment, you experience the highest expression of your defined centers, and you are a confident and consistent way-shower. When you are out of alignment, you can experience the lowest expression; you might be shy to be seen and avoidant of your truth. In the highest expression of your undefined centers, you are a wise and discerning empath. In the lowest expression, you are confusing what you feel from others as your own feelings, causing further misalignment and not-self. Here is a breakdown of what each of the centers means, along with the highest and lowest expressions of its defined and undefined modes of operation.

Head Center

Pressure Center

PRESSURE TO "KNOW" THAT DRIVES OUR THINKING

THE CENTER OF ASKING QUESTIONS and inspiration

PHYSICAL ASSOCIATION: the pineal gland

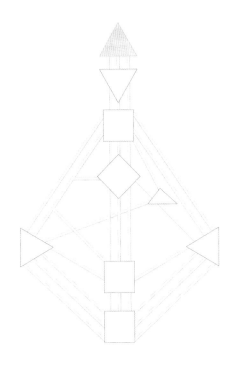

DEFINED

30% of the population has consistent mental pressure to ask inspired questions about and comprehend life.

- **HIGH VIBE:** Self-inspired. Inspires others mentally and asks questions about life to help the world evolve forward.
- **LOW VIBE:** Turning mental pressure inward, causing anxiety, self-doubt, and confusion. Aggressively forcing their opinions, questions, and pressure on others. Not using S&A for timing to share ideas.

UNDEFINED

70% of the population has no consistent way of thinking or pressure to ask questions.

- **HIGH VIBE:** Open-minded and inspired by the world around them. Able to sense and understand what others are thinking. Has discernment for whose thoughts are inspiring and helpful right now.
- **LOW VIBE:** Overwhelmed by mental pressure. Doesn't want to get involved in intellectual conversations. Worried about things that don't matter. Trying to solve other people's problems all the time. Always searching for who has the answers.

Ajna Center

Awareness Center

MENTAL AWARENESS

THE CENTER OF ANSWERING QUESTIONS, opinions, forming ideas

PHYSICAL ASSOCIATIONS: pituitary glands

DEFINED

47% of the population has a consistent way of thinking that influences the world around them and will hone their own point of view over time.

- **HIGH VIBE:** Enjoys mental stimulation and creativity. Allows themselves to be a thought leader.
- **LOW VIBE:** Is dependent on their mind for decisions and obsesses over small actions. Afraid to share their thoughts and opinions. Overthinks. Obsesses over things that it is too late to take action on.

UNDEFINED

53% of the population is designed to be open-minded and able to take in and entertain a wide range of concepts.

- **HIGH VIBE:** Open-minded and flexible opinions. Senses what others are thinking and who has the answers. Has discernment for what opinions matter right now.
- **LOW VIBE:** Feels pressure to seem certain. Clings to ideas or opinions to feel more secure. Does not want to share their discernment of what matters right now. Avoids intellectual conversations.

Throat Center

Manifestation Center

COMMUNICATION

THE CENTER OF EXTERNALIZING, expressing self, and manifesting

PHYSICAL ASSOCIATIONS: thyroid

DEFINED

72% of the population has a consistent way of using their voice to express
themselves.

- **HIGH VIBE:** Has a consistent ability
  to communicate their truth and has
  perfect timing for sharing when in
  alignment with their S&A.
- **LOW VIBE:** Quiets their voice to fit in. Doesn't use their S&A and is pushy or
  repels with what they say.
  Feels their voice doesn't matter. Plays small.

UNDEFINED

28% of the population is an advocate and voice for something outside of themselves but is inconsistent when talking about themselves.

- **HIGH VIBE:** Confidently listens when they don't want to speak, shares when
  they do, and gives a voice to the voiceless. Enjoys having many different
  voices and ways of expressing themselves.
- **LOW VIBE:** Feels a need to attract attention or feels unheard, which leads to
  yelling or interrupting. Tries to make something happen that isn't actually
  important to them or their S&A. Feels unnoticed or unimportant. Forces
  themselves to speak or share to fill the silence.

G Center

Identity Center

IDENTITY AND SELF-DIRECTION

THE CENTER OF LOVE, connection to
   higher self, and the magnetic mono-
   pole (a magnet that attracts you to
   your aligned path)

PHYSICAL ASSOCIATIONS: the liver and the
   blood

DEFINED

57% of the population has a fixed
self-identity and a consistent life
direction.

- **HIGH VIBE:** Has a consistent sense of
  who they are and what they love. Independent and focused on their mission
  and their own direction in life.
- **LOW VIBE:** Bends who they are or dims their light to fit in with others. Tries
  to force others to go in the same direction as them.

UNDEFINED

43% of the population has an inconsistent sense of self-identity and personal
direction.

- **HIGH VIBE:** Adaptable and receptive to different people and environments.
  Can see others' life paths clearly and can give excellent advice. Enjoys having
  many interests and a fluid personal direction when aligned with their S&A.
- **LOW VIBE:** Grips on to other people's direction. Feels unloved and lost in life.
  Relies on others to show them who they are.

Ego/Heart Center

Motor (Energy) Center

MOTOR THAT DRIVES WILLPOWER

THE CENTER OF MOTIVATION, material world desires, and self-worth

PHYSICAL ASSOCIATIONS: the heart and the digestive system

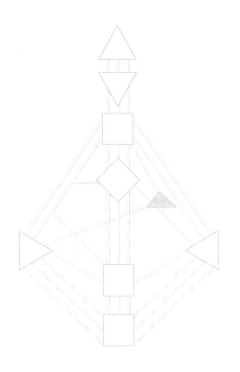

DEFINED

37% of the population has consistent motivation and power needed to have control over their life and resources.

- **HIGH VIBE:** Has a healthy sense of their own value. Can commit and follow through on things by using their S&A.
- **LOW VIBE:** Forces things and places high expectations on others. Is overly competitive. Pushes themselves and others too hard.

UNDEFINED

63% of the population has inconsistent motivation and willpower.

- **HIGH VIBE:** Trusts that they have the exact amount of motivation they need and honors the times they are not motivated without pushing themselves. Doesn't need to know what they want all the time.
- **LOW VIBE:** Always trying to prove themselves. Lacks self-worth and under-estimates their own value. Feels unworthy. Forces their own motivation and willpower to the point of burnout.

Splenic Center

Awareness Center

BODY AWARENESS

THE CENTER OF INSTINCTS, intuition, safety, fear, and health

PHYSICAL ASSOCIATIONS: the immune system, lymphatic system, and spleen

DEFINED

55% of the population has consistent and reliable instincts and intuition.

- **HIGH VIBE:** Trusts their body's intelligence. Listens to their instincts and intuition in the present moment. Is able to make spontaneous judgments about what is healthy and safe.
- **LOW VIBE:** Lets fear hold them back from trusting themselves or hearing their own intuition.

UNDEFINED

45% of the population is empathetic to the fears, anxiety, health, and instincts of others. Has inconsistent personal intuition and safety instincts.

- **HIGH VIBE:** Trusts their intuition about others. Can sense who is healthy and well and who is not.
- **LOW VIBE:** Is overly dependent on others. Feels unsafe. Holds on to other people's fear or illness as their own.

Solar Plexus Center

Awareness Center and Motor (Energy) Center

EMOTIONAL AWARENESS

A MOTOR THAT PROVIDES THE DRIVE
to feel and connect

THE CENTER OF EMOTIONS, spirit
consciousness, passion, romance,
and desire

PHYSICAL ASSOCIATIONS: the nervous system, lungs, pancreas, prostate,
and kidneys

DEFINED

53% of the population creates and experiences their own emotional wave.

- **HIGH VIBE:** Cultivates emotional intelligence over time. Develops depth,
  resilience, and maturity through accepting and embracing the highs and
  lows of their wave and waiting to find clarity.
- **LOW VIBE:** Looks for external circumstances to justify their emotions. Is
  impulsive with emotionally charged decisions and unaware of their emotional wave.

UNDEFINED

47% of the population empathetically experiences an amplified version of other
people's emotions in their own being.

- **HIGH VIBE:** Has discernment between what emotions are their own and what
  emotions belong to others. Compassionately observes and supports the
  emotional health of others.
- **LOW VIBE:** Identifies with emotions that aren't their own. Is afraid of emotions and avoids confrontation. Is unaware of their own emotional empathy.

Sacral Center

Motor (Energy) Center

A MOTOR THAT GENERATES LIFE-FORCE ENERGY

THE CENTER OF CREATIVE ENERGY, sexuality, fertility, and guiding life through response

PHYSICAL ASSOCIATIONS: sexual organs

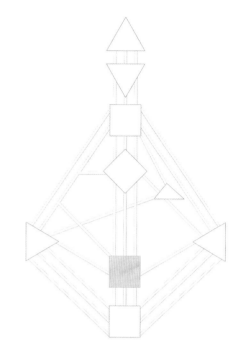

DEFINED

66% of the population
creates their own energy to sustainably
fuel themselves each day.

- **HIGH VIBE:** Uses creative energy to work on what they love. Listens to their sacral responses to guide them toward what to use their energy on.
- **LOW VIBE:** Gives their energy away doing what they "should" do. Sacrifices themselves for others.

UNDEFINED

34% of the population does not create a sustainable source of consistent energy. Gets fuel by feeding off the energy of others.

- **HIGH VIBE:** Works less and rests when they are tired. Knows when enough is enough.
- **LOW VIBE:** Consistently overworks. Tries to be consistent and keep up with others. Burns themselves out.

Root Center

Pressure Center and Motor (Energy) Center

PROVIDES PRESSURE AND FUEL TO TAKE
 ACTION AND MOVE FORWARD
THE CENTER OF STRESS, momentum,
 and adaptation
PHYSICAL ASSOCIATION: the adrenal glands

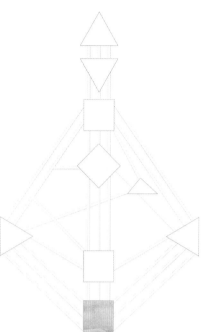

DEFINED

60% of the population has a consistent
way of handling stress and pressure to
move things forward.

- HIGH VIBE: Is calm and grounded in
  stressful situations. Works well under
  pressure. Has a consistent way of getting things done.
- LOW VIBE: Ignores S&A, thus generating stress for themselves. Initiates
  unimportant tasks and meets resistance along the way. Pressures others
  to do more and meet unrealistic expectations.

UNDEFINED

40% of the population is open to receiving pressure that fuels them in getting
things done.

- HIGH VIBE: Trusts that things will get done when they need to and doesn't
  force things. Has discernment with what pressure is their own or not.
- LOW VIBE: Is restless, is overwhelmed by stress, and tries to do everything
  to relieve pressure. Feels there is always something to do.

Undefined Centers: Not-Self Talk to Highest-Self Talk Cheat Sheet

Although it is possible to be in the lowest expression of your defined centers, being in the lowest expression of your undefined centers is far more common and central to keeping us in our not-self. We have created this cheat sheet to help you notice when you might be in the lowest expression of your undefined centers along with mantras to help you come back into alignment.

You may be in your not-self if you have one of the below centers undefined and you find yourself saying:	Transmute the lower vibration by saying one of these affirmations aloud.
THE UNDEFINED CENTERS: *Not-Self Talk*	**THE UNDEFINED CENTERS:** *Highest-Self Talk*

Undefined Head Center

"I have to find something that is inspiring."	"I allow the answers to come to me in divine timing."
"Where can I go for answers?"	"I do not need to know yet."
"I have to make sense of this."	"I am brilliant at understanding how others think."

Undefined Ajna Center

"I need to know the answers and be more certain."	"I am open-minded."
"I need to figure out what I'm going to do next so my life is not so chaotic."	"I can see through other people's perspectives and find the way forward."
"Will people think I am strange if I share this idea?"	"I release certainty and embrace possibility and flexibility."

THE UNDEFINED CENTERS: Not-Self Talk	THE UNDEFINED CENTERS: Highest-Self Talk
Undefined Throat Center	
"Does anyone see me?"	"I am an advocate for others."
"If I say this, I will get attention."	"I give a voice to the voiceless."
"If I start a conversation, I will get noticed more."	"I can sense others' needs."
	"I am confident in my timing."
	"I am comfortable in silence."
Undefined G Center	
"I wish I knew my thing."	"I am here."
"Where can I go and who can help me discover who I am?"	"I see others."
"Who will love me for me and where is my soul mate?"	"I don't need to know where I am going."
	"I am designed to have lots of interests."
Undefined Ego/Heart Center	
"I have to earn my worth."	"I have nothing to prove."
"Am I trying to prove that I can do this?"	"I am inherently worthy."
"Am I forcing myself to be hardworking to seem valuable?"	"I'm not designed to have consistent motivation."
Undefined Splenic Center	
"I am afraid of doing that, of the responsibility, or of the outcome."	"I release fear."
"Am I holding onto things that are not good for me?"	"I trust myself to feel what's not good for me."
"I do not feel safe on my own."	

THE UNDEFINED CENTERS: | THE UNDEFINED CENTERS:

Not-Self Talk | *Highest-Self Talk*

Undefined Solar Plexus Center

"I can't say that because it might be upsetting."	"I am brilliantly empathetic."
"It's not worth it to go there, say this, or do this thing."	"I have emotional discernment."
"How can I best avoid confrontation?"	"I can clear emotions I've picked up at any time."

Undefined Sacral Center

"There is just too much to do to rest right now."	"Rest = success."
"I'd better say yes or I might miss out on something."	"I set healthy boundaries."
"If I don't do it, no one will."	
"Who and what can I be taking care of right now?"	

Undefined Root Center

"I have to hurry up and get all of these things done now."	"I release the pressure to do everything."
"There is no time to waste."	"I am grounded."
"I have to always start or search for new experiences."	"I embrace help from others."
"Where can I go and who can I be around to be needed?"	
"I could be doing more."	

CHAPTER 7

Deeper Dive: Profiles

YOUR PROFILE IN HUMAN DESIGN DESCRIBES your personality archetype. Whereas your Type is how people experience your energy on an energetic level, your Profile is how people experience you consciously. It is composed of two numbers. The first number (on the left) is the conscious side of your personality that you can really see in yourself. The second number (on the right) is unconscious for you and is what other people see in you the most. These two numbers give you a polarity and balance within your personality. They are why you might sometimes feel "Who am I? Am I this side or that?" and the truth is, you are both!

There are twelve different Profiles. Every person is one of the 12. They are: 1/3, 1/4, 2/4, 2/5, 3/5, 3/6, 4/1, 4/6, 5/1, 5/2, 6/2, and 6/3. Each Profile is composed of two lines from the six lines of the hexagram.

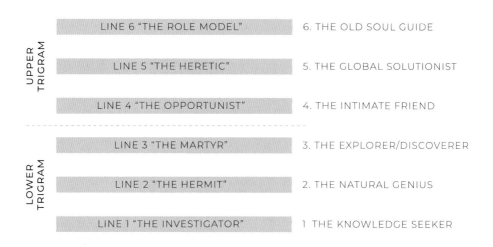

UPPER TRIGRAM	LINE 6 "THE ROLE MODEL"	6. THE OLD SOUL GUIDE
	LINE 5 "THE HERETIC"	5. THE GLOBAL SOLUTIONIST
	LINE 4 "THE OPPORTUNIST"	4. THE INTIMATE FRIEND
LOWER TRIGRAM	LINE 3 "THE MARTYR"	3. THE EXPLORER/DISCOVERER
	LINE 2 "THE HERMIT"	2. THE NATURAL GENIUS
	LINE 1 "THE INVESTIGATOR"	1 THE KNOWLEDGE SEEKER

The 6 Lines of the Hexagram

LINE 1: THE INVESTIGATOR (THE KNOWLEDGE SEEKER*)

The investigator is here to seek information, study the world (including people's behaviors), and create a completely solid foundation of knowledge and eventually become an authority. The best way they learn is through studying and preparing.

LINE 2: THE HERMIT (THE NATURAL GENIUS*)

The hermit is here to have natural talent (although they can't always see what their talents are), and others who can see their talents can call on them to share. They prefer a lot of alone time with which to relax and be creative doing their own thing, in their own space, uninterrupted. The best way they learn is through following what comes naturally to them and teaching what they already know.

LINE 3: THE MARTYR (THE EXPLORER/DISCOVERER*)

The martyr is here to learn through experiential trial and error. They are here to jump in, try things out, bump into new discoveries along the way, and help the world find mutation and progress. They often receive blame (especially as children) for making mistakes. They are quickest to find what doesn't work and to call out those things. They are here to cultivate the ability to set healthy boundaries. The best way they learn is through physically trying something.

LINE 4: THE OPPORTUNIST (THE INTIMATE FRIEND*)

The opportunist is here to connect in an intimate, deep, and authentic way. They are gifted at socializing in a friendly, warm manner, and they are interested in building close relationships which are often where their greatest opportunities naturally come from. They thrive with stability. The best way they teach or connect is in close and authentic ways.

LINE 5: THE HERETIC (THE GLOBAL SOLUTIONIST*)

The heretic is here to create workable solutions that help others and share universalized messages that can reach a wide range of people. Their energy naturally contains a projection field that elicits judgments from others. They have a strong desire to save others, so it's up to them to cultivate a clear sense of self, and to agree to help only when they are certain they can and when it's aligned with their S&A to do so. If they give in to the pressure they feel from others to be who people think they are, they can end up damaging their reputation. The best way they teach or connect is through universal concepts, problems, and solutions.

LINE 6: THE ROLE MODEL (THE OLD SOUL GUIDE*)

The role model is here to help guide others into becoming their most authentic selves. The best way they do this is by modeling authenticity. They feel the best when they get to have some space for observing and being objective, instead of being overinvolved. The role model acts as a martyr (3 Line) when they are under thirty years old. At age thirty, they begin transitioning into embodying more of the 6 line energy and at age fifty they become the most recognized as a role model. The best way they teach and connect is by example and with a bit of space and objectivity.

These terms are ones we have come up with to quickly communicate the essence of each archetype. Note: To see where you can discover your Profile on your Human Design chart, see page 17.

What Your Profile Indicates

We came up with these terms to quickly communicate the essence of each archtype.

1/3 PROFILE: THE KNOWLEDGE SEEKER / THE EXPLORER / DISCOVERER
The lifelong student who becomes a mentor

- Someone with a 1/3 Profile balances their need to cautiously investigate first and their need to jump in and try it out.

- They can struggle with imposter syndrome when stepping into teaching because they feel there is always more to learn.

- They are gifted at feeling when something is off in a relationship and are here to enforce boundaries or space.

- They are empathetic and gifted at studying people. They can tell when people are lying or being inauthentic.

1/4 PROFILE: THE KNOWLEDGE SEEKER / THE INTIMATE FRIEND
The deeply curious investigator who wants to share everything they discover

- Someone with a 1/4 Profile balances their need to cautiously investigate alone first with their desire to immediately share and learn within a close and deeply connected friend group, community, or family.

- Super friendly and warm, they are gifted at making others feel comfortable, building close bonds, and helping people open up.

- They are very interested in human behavior and understanding people.

- The quality of their well-being depends on the quality of their closest relationships.

2/4 PROFILE: THE NATURAL GENIUS / THE INTIMATE FRIEND
The considerate, introverted extravert

- Someone with a 2/4 Profile balances their need for alone time with their need for social time within close community.

- They are gifted at holding space for others and intuitively sensing their needs. They are easygoing and democratic.

- They have natural talents but are unaware of what they are or how to explain them to others.

- Others see their talents and call them out to share.

- It is important that they feel close to those they work with.

- When they answer a correct call, they can have a powerful driving force that externalizes their mission.

2/5 PROFILE: THE NATURAL GENIUS / THE GLOBAL SOLUTIONIST

The unassuming natural who could lead a revolution

- Someone with a 2/5 Profile balances their need for alone time with their desire to lead the world toward a better future.

- They are not aware of their alluring personality, their natural talents, or how to explain them, but others see them really well and call them out to be shared.

- They are creative and gifted at self-marketing when they are clear about their mission in the world.

- They have a projection field of others expecting them to be what they want them to be or to help when they want them to.

3/5 PROFILE: THE EXPLORER / DISCOVERER / THE GLOBAL SOLUTIONIST

The intriguing and adventurous activist

- Someone with a 3/5 Profile balances their desire to just explore and do their own thing with their desire to lead the world toward a better future.

- They are here to call out what is not right or not fair and offer solutions.

- They must try things on their own to see whether or not it works for them.

- They attract a life full of experiences that are really interesting to others.

- They have a sensitivity to when others need support but also have a projection field that blocks others from seeing when they need support.

3/6 PROFILE: THE EXPLORER / DISCOVERER / THE OLD SOUL GUIDE

The responsible and chill adventurer

- Someone with a 3/6 Profile balances their desire to just go out and explore new things with their desire to stay put, be responsible, and support/guide others.

- They learn completely through trial and error when young, but they also have an old soul/perfectionist energy from the 6 line that doesn't like making "mistakes."

- They want to experience firsthand but also want to sit back and observe.

- They are nourished by having both a home to nest in and some freedom to travel and explore.

4/1 PROFILE: THE INTIMATE FRIEND/THE KNOWLEDGE SEEKER

The playful psychologist who is here to study life

- Someone with a 4/1 Profile balances their need for social time sharing in a close community with their need to investigate on their own.

- They are extremely rare and are the only Profile that has a Juxtaposition Cross of Incarnation. They are here to bring depth and curiosity to life mixed with a lightness and playfulness.

- They are deeply interested in human behavior.

- They have a strong, fixed way of living and are not meant to bend themselves for a relationship.

- They can undergo a huge change at some point in their life.

4/6 PROFILE: THE INTIMATE FRIEND / THE OLD SOUL GUIDE

The humanitarian and mind-expanding guide of their group

- Someone with a 4/6 Profile balances their need for time sharing in intimate close relationships with their desire to help others but in a removed way.

- They can struggle with heart vs. head or with spiritual/trusting vs. logical/observant/cautious.

- They can be perfectionists and hate making mistakes when they are young and in their trial and error/3 line stage.

- They can take longer to become dependent. It's important for them to receive support, although it can feel uncomfortable for them to do so.

- Later in life, they often help the collective in a big way.

5/1 PROFILE: THE GLOBAL SOLUTIONIST/THE KNOWLEDGE SEEKER

The intriguing global solutionist and the mysterious wild card

- Someone with a 5/1 Profile balances educating and directing the world toward a better future with feeling like there is always more to learn before doing so.

- Deeply curious, they want to investigate and build knowledge and skills to share with the world.

- They have a seductive projection field that makes others see them being who they want them to be.

- They can tarnish their reputation if they try to fulfill misaligned expectations.

- They operate best when they spend ample time self-reflecting.

5/2 PROFILE: THE GLOBAL SOLUTIONIST/THE NATURAL GENIUS

The brilliant rebel who can lead a revolution, but only on their own terms

- Someone with a 5/2 Profile balances their desire to lead the world toward a better future with their need for alone time they can use to do their own thing with no pressure.

- They can receive a lot of recognition around their gifts and can be pressured to "do something" with them.

- It's crucial that they only take action or decide to use their gifts because they truly are motivated to do so on their own.

6/2 PROFILE: THE OLD SOUL GUIDE/THE NATURAL GENIUS

The boss old soul who role-models authenticity

- Someone with a 6/2 Profiles balances their desire to be responsible and guide or support others with their desire to be alone to do their own thing.

- They have natural talents that they are not aware of or can't explain, but others see them easily and call them out to be shared.

- They can be idealistic or perfectionist, and they hate making mistakes when they are young and in their trial and error/3 line stage.

- They don't like petty drama, but they do crave deep experiences on a soul level, including finding a soul mate.

- They have a humanitarian heart and a hopeful, supportive outlook for others, but they don't want to have to hold people's hand.

6/3 PROFILE: THE OLD SOUL GUIDE / THE EXPLORER / DISCOVERER

The exciting adventurer turned responsible guide

- Someone with a 6/3 Profile balances their desire to be settled, responsible, and supportive of others with their desire to go out and explore exciting new things.

- They want to nest at home but also get restless to go travel and explore.

- They thrive when taking on extreme experiences or when they need to step up to the plate and handle something.

- They are always designed to learn through trial and error, but when they are young, they can have an old soul perfectionism that hates making mistakes.

- They thrive when they have trusted relationships that support their need for freedom to explore.

Understanding your Profile can help you have balance and harmony in your day-to-day life and relationships. You are not designed to favor one side of your personality over the other. You are designed to embrace both sides in a harmonious but not necessarily equal mixture. Having awareness of both sides of your personality allows you to bring yourself back to balance, easing the resistance in your life and supporting your alignment.

CHAPTER 8

Deeper Dive: Channels and Gates

.

O N YOUR CHART, YOU WILL SEE a bodygraph with triangular and square energy centers, as well as colored lines that connect those centers and half lines reaching out from a center. Those lines and half lines are called channels and gates, and they represent your inherent energetic traits. If a line or half line is colored in black, it is a conscious trait for you—a trait that you will easily recognize in yourself. If a line or half line is colored in red, it is an unconscious trait for you—a trait that is equally important but less apparent to you. If a line or half line is striped both black and red, that trait is both conscious and unconscious and is extra prominent in your chart.

If you have a black or red half line reaching out from a center that doesn't fully connect to another center, it is a gate. If you have a black or red line that fully connects two centers, it is a channel. A single channel is made up of two gates— two energetic qualities—coming together to form a synthesis of these qualities. A red half line that meets a black half line is a channel where half is unconscious and half is conscious. The numbers on either side of a channel are the numbers of the gates that join together to form that channel. Each of the 36 channels has a slightly different meaning from the sum of their two parts, but we won't get into that here. You can begin to get an understanding of the energetic qualities a channel holds by combining the meanings of the two gates that comprise it.

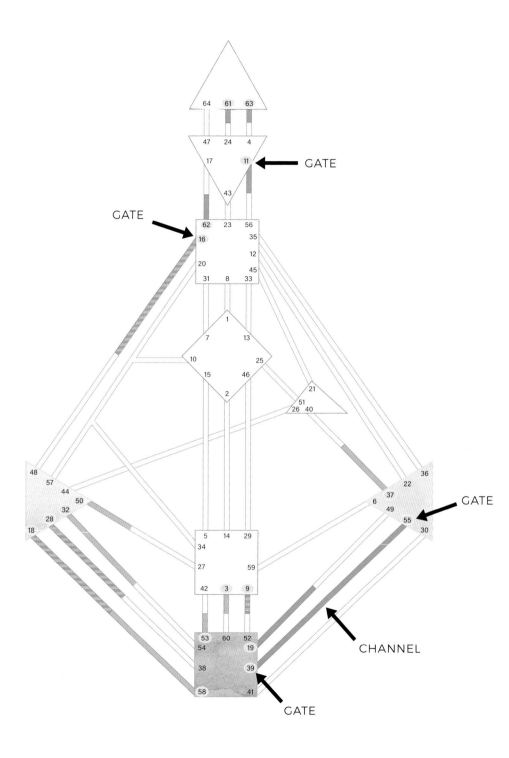

GATE

GATE

GATE

CHANNEL

GATE

Your channels and gates are your natural energetic qualities and gifts. You are here to use them in everything that you do. When you have a job, project, career, or relationship that allows you to use some of your gates and channels, you feel good about it. Over time, however, you might feel as though something is missing, you're burnt out, or it's not what you thought it was. This is because you are not showing up as your full self, using all of your gifts. Simply having awareness of your inherent characteristics is powerful, in and of itself, but you can also attract more opportunities for which you can naturally use all of your gifts by practicing your Strategy and Authority.

Each channel or gate has a highest expression and a lowest expression, a superpower and a fear, and an outer expression and an inner expression. In this chapter, we offer some affirmations for embodying the highest expression of each gate to help you understand and work with your unique energy. For a deeper dive into all of the channels and gates to fully understand the highest and lowest expressions, we recommend exploring our online channel videos on daylunalife. com or booking a Human Design reading.

Gate Affirmations

Find all of your gates below and say these affirmations aloud to support your highest expression. If you have a channel, find both gates in that channel, because both affirmations apply to you.

GATE 1: I express my authentic self through my ideas and creations.

GATE 2: I understand the correct resources needed to support and actualize a creative dream.

GATE 3: I am wise when helping reorder a situation to find a new perspective.

GATE 4: I use my logic to create solutions and formulas.

GATE 5: I nurture myself with routines and rituals that connect me to life's natural rhythm.

GATE 6: I find the people who are right for me by provoking intimacy.

GATE 7: I am a powerful and loving alpha leader.

GATE 8: I inspire others by sharing my unique taste, exciting ideas, and creations.

GATE 9: I hone in on important details others might miss.

GATE 10: I cultivate and model self-love.

GATE 11: I constantly channel interesting ideas.

GATE 12: I share poetically only when I am in the mood to do so.

GATE 13: I cultivate wisdom through listening with compassion and receptivity.

GATE 14: I am a good luck charm for resources and success and naturally bring out the best in others.

GATE 15: I embrace the extremes within my own natural daily life rhythms and model a love and acceptance for diversity in humanity.

GATE 16: I have powerful physical skills and talents that I develop and share with excitement.

GATE 17: I share my opinions with confidence.

GATE 18: I enjoy being the authority over my own life and am gifted at making corrections and improvements.

GATE 19: I can sense what people need on a physical and spiritual level.

GATE 20: I tune in to the present moment and speak the truth with love.

GATE 21: I have a natural talent for controlling finances and other resources.

GATE 22: I have graceful timing.

GATE 23: I assimilate complicated ideas and communicate them in a way that is easy to understand.

GATE 24: I am a thinker who revisits mental concepts over and over again to find truth.

GATE 25: I cultivate and exude a spiritual love for all beings and see all of life as worthy of love.

GATE 26: I am a persuasive communicator and can explain things in a way that puts others at ease.

GATE 27: I am a natural nurturer.

GATE 28: I embrace living life to the fullest by taking on meaningful risks.

GATE 29: I learn deep lessons through committing my energy to meaningful experiences and connecting deeply with others.

GATE 30: My soul craves emotional depth.

GATE 31: I influence others and lead by example.

GATE 32: I sense which projects and processes are going to succeed and which are not.

GATE 33: I am a wise observer who needs space to reflect.

GATE 34: I inspire others when I do what I love and share my authentic self.

GATE 35: I initiate growth in the lives of others by sharing my own emotional memories and experiences.

GATE 36: I navigate and transform my own emotional challenges and help others to do the same.

GATE 37: I help my friends, family, and community gather together with my warm presence.

GATE 38: I am willing to take on meaningful challenges in order to stand up for causes and ideals I believe in.

GATE 39: My energy stimulates the mutation and up-leveling of consciousness in others.

GATE 40: I am willing to give to my friends, family, and community when I am doing work I love.

GATE 41: I am a dreamer who wants to creatively express what I feel when I'm deeply moved by life.

GATE 42: I help guide growth by looking at conclusions from the past.

GATE 43: I have progressive, unique insight.

GATE 44: I understand life's patterns and can break unhealthy cycles.

GATE 45: I compassionately direct my community toward abundance.

GATE 46: I help others find appreciation and love for their body by honoring my own.

GATE 47: I receive powerful revelations that come to me in their own timing.

GATE 48: I have a depth that allows me to see what is needed for the collective to be supported.

GATE 49: I am of service in alignment with my humanitarian principles.

GATE 50: I take responsibility for leading my community by infusing my values and integrity into all I do.

GATE 51: I help shock and awaken others.

GATE 52: I find meditative stillness and flow-zone focus when working on something I love.

GATE 53: My energy fuels growth and change in the world around me.

GATE 54: I am driven to build something exciting that provides for me and my family.

GATE 55: I feel a profound emotional and spiritual connection to the full spectrum of life's hope and pain.

GATE 56: I share my personal perspective on the meaning of life in an interesting way.

GATE 57: I have instinctual insight that guides me moment to moment toward a healthy future.

GATE 58: I have a natural, vibrant enthusiasm for making life better.

GATE 59: My energy helps people feel closeness.

GATE 60: I transcend limitations when I can and acccpt them when I can't.

GATE 61: I dive into contemplating life's esoteric mysteries.

GATE 62: I teach by presenting details and facts in an organized, clear way.

GATE 63: I question the things that seem off in the world around me to find what's real.

GATE 64: I can dive into deep and confusing mental topics to find clarity and understanding.

CHAPTER 9

Deeper Dive: Cross of Incarnation

Y OUR CROSS OF INCARNATION TELLS YOU what your life purpose is in this lifetime. When we think of our life purpose, we often think it is something we came here to do. We are often asked something like, "I am really interested in life coaching; is that my life purpose?" or "I am studying to become a doctor; is that my life purpose?" Your life purpose is not any one thing you came here to do, but instead it is the energy you came here to be in all of the things you do, in every iteration of your career, and through every iteration of who you are throughout this lifetime.

Ra Uru Hu says, "You awaken IN your Cross of Incarnation." Through using your Strategy and Authority, you increase your magnetism and attract opportunities in which you can naturally be this energy in the world, and you can look back and see that this energy was in all the things you were doing. This is the gift you came to bring for others, for projects, and for yourself.

Your Cross of Incarnation is arguably one of the most important aspects of your Human Design (other than Strategy and Authority) because it comprises your most prominent gifts—your Sun gates and your Earth gates.

There are 192 basic crosses of incarnation, so you really are incredibly unique compared to others who may have your same Type or Authority. To start leaning in to your unique life purpose more, we recommend saying your Sun gate and Earth gate affirmations aloud each day.

To understand aspects of your Cross of Incarnation, you can learn about your Sun and Earth gates look up your specific cross or get a reading. There are many resources online and through our website, daylunalife.com, to help you.

Type: **Projector**

Profile: **2/4**

Definition: **Triple Split Definition**

Inner Authority: **Emotional - Solar Plexus**

Strategy: **Wait for the Invitation**

Not-Self Theme: **Bitterness**

Incarnation Cross: **Right Angle Cross of Contagion (29/30 | 8/14)**

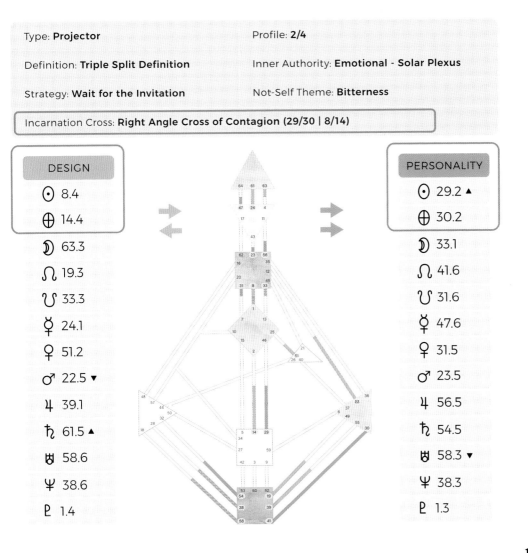

DESIGN		PERSONALITY	
☉ 8.4		☉ 29.2 ▲	
⊕ 14.4		⊕ 30.2	
☽ 63.3		☽ 33.1	
☊ 19.3		☊ 41.6	
☋ 33.3		☋ 31.6	
☿ 24.1		☿ 47.6	
♀ 51.2		♀ 31.5	
♂ 22.5 ▼		♂ 23.5	
♃ 39.1		♃ 56.5	
♄ 61.5 ▲		♄ 54.5	
♅ 58.6		♅ 58.3 ▼	
♆ 38.6		♆ 38.3	
♇ 1.4		♇ 1.3	

CHAPTER 10

Tying It All Together

Y OUR HUMAN DESIGN CHART IS COMPLEX, and sometimes understanding it can be overwhelming. Our goal is to simplify your Human Design journey so you can use it in a way that gives you powerful results and a life-changing understanding of self.

How to Further Explore Your Human Design

We recommend exploring your Human Design in this order to get the most out of it.

1. START WITH UNDERSTANDING
YOUR TYPE, STRATEGY, AND AUTHORITY

Reflect on times you have felt these themes and what specific information is resonating for you right now in your life. Start observing your day-to-day life with the awareness of how your body is feeling and where your energy levels are. Then set an amount of time (two weeks to one month) and use it to experiment with really leaning in to your daily practice and making every big decision with your Authority.

2. ADD IN DECONDITIONING AROUND YOUR OPEN CENTERS

Once you have been using your S&A for a few weeks, start observing any of the not-self talk that you resonate with from the center's cheat sheet and catch yourself. It is as simple as noticing when you are in the lowest expression and choosing to then say the affirmation listed to help you move toward the highest expression in that moment.

3. ADD IN UNDERSTANDING YOUR PROFILE

Start observing both sides of your Profile and explore learning and teaching through your specific style. When you are feeling off balance, lean in to the side of your Profile you may have been ignoring and feel whether it brings more harmony to your energy field.

4. LEARN ABOUT YOUR SPECIFIC CHANNELS, GATES, AND CROSS OF INCARNATION

Start saying your gate affirmations aloud to yourself to really see yourself and celebrate your highest expression. Explore your channels through our video courses or with a personalized reading. Reflect on times or areas of your life in which you are already using these gifts. The magic happens when you see that you already are these energies and that you do not have to do anything to prove you have these gifts.

How to Keep Going on Your Human Design Journey

There are many facets to Human Design, because there are many facets to us as individuals. Once you have been practicing some of the teachings in this book and honoring your Human Design, we recommend going even deeper into your self-discovery.

GET A READING

Having a personalized Human Design reading is powerful! We cannot say that enough. It is priceless to have someone hold up a mirror of your energy and reflect back your unique gifts, how you are currently using them, and how you can go even further. This is also the best way to understand your Cross of Incarnation and your life purpose.

DISCOVER YOUR PRIMARY HEALTH SYSTEM

Your Primary Health System (PHS) details the energetically correct diet, environment, and mind-set that is best for you. This is fascinating to experiment with, but it is important for you to fully understand your Strategy and Authority first. If your S&A says no to any aspect of your PHS, that is your truth and means that your highest alignment right now is to not follow your PHS and to keep focusing on deconditioning. Eating in your diet and living in your environment will set you up for better health and more success and abundance in your life.

BECOME A HUMAN DESIGN READER

Learn everything you need to start offering readings for your friends, family, and even clients to take your Human Design journey to the next level. We offer an array of classes and video courses for you to explore on daylunalife.com.

Our biggest advice? Experiment, experiment, experiment! You are the only person who can feel whether these teachings and practices are meaningful and helpful for you. You are here to be your own authority. No person, business, teaching, or organization is here to control your life or tell you what is true for you, so we invite you to reflect, observe, and explore to see how this information supports you or doesn't. After well over a thousand readings, we have seen this powerful system transform each person's life in deeply profound ways.

Your highest potential is waiting for you. Are you ready to dive in?

About the Authors

DANA STILES AND SHAYNA CORNELIUS are the Human Design specialists, spiritual teachers, and podcast hosts behind Day-Luna™. As cofounders and owners of their company, they are on a mission to empower the collective toward self-love, personal freedom, and radical authenticity.

After meeting in college more than fourteen years ago, together they have experienced many beautiful adventures, including their spiritual awakening. When Dana and Shayna discovered Human Design, just before their Saturn Returns, they were both working in traditional corporate careers. They were trying to fit into the homogenized world, exhausting their energy, feeling a longing for something more, and passionately studying spirituality in their free time. During their journeys, Shayna and Dana heard about Human Design. When they began learning about their own unique designs (they are both 2/4 Projectors!), the powerful revelations they discovered became a catalyst that radically changed every aspect of their lives. They felt a burning passion to fully commit to living by their design and to understand every single facet of this complex spiritual science. That journey quickly led them to quit their secure, traditional jobs and answer a divine calling to spread the wisdom that is Human Design.

Through their soul-centered business DayLuna™, which launched in 2019, Dana and Shayna specialize in the realm of self-purpose and conscious entrepreneurship and have been very successful in guiding their clients. Through DayLuna™, they have worked with more than 1,000 clients and have trained many to become readers themselves. The pair feel passionately called to help spread the complex and life-changing science of Human Design to a wider community in a grounded and approachable way. With testimonials stating, "By far the best I have come across," "Extremely thorough," and "[They] set the bar high and delivered," it is clear they are doing just that. In addition to their readings, DayLuna™ services and offerings include personalized ritual kits, video courses, trainings, meditation tools, and more—all centered around an individual's Human Design and astrology.

Dana and Shayna also share their knowledge by deep diving into topics such as spirituality, parenting, and the new paradigm as the cohosts of the *DayLuna™ Human Design Podcast*, a show created to teach about Human Design and help empower others to dive into their own personal power through self-awareness.

When they aren't working, Shayna enjoys traveling in her Airstream and going to the beach with her dogs, while Dana enjoys snowboarding, singing, and practicing kundalini yoga. The pair are both currently living and thriving in California, while working on several large new offerings to continue empowering others toward their highest potential.

Index

Affirmations, Gate, 161–164
Ajna Center, 138, 146
auras, 9–10
authorities
    about, 91–92
    Ego-Manifested Authority, 113–117, 131
    Ego-Projected Authority, 109–112, 132
    Emotional Authority, 92–100, 130, 131, 132
    Lunar Authority, 125–129, 133
    Mental/Environmental Authority, 121–125, 132
    Sacral Authority, 101–104, 131–132
    Self-Projected/G Center Authority, 117–120, 132
    Splenic Authority, 105–108, 131, 132
    strategy and, 130–133, 169

Book of Changes, The (I Ching), 13, 15

centers
    about, 135–136
    Ajna Center, 138, 146
    Ego/Heart Center, 141, 147
    G Center, 140, 147
    Head Center, 137, 146
    Root Center, 145, 148
    Sacral Center, 144, 148
    Solar Plexus Center, 143, 148
    Splenic Center, 142, 147
    Throat Center, 139, 147
    undefined, 146–148
chakra system, 13–14
channels, 159–161, 170
codons, 15
conditioning, 10
Cross of Incarnation, 166–167, 170

deconditioning, 11, 170
DNA, 15

Ego/Heart Center, 141, 147
Ego-Manifested Authority, 113–117, 131
Ego-Projected Authority, 109–112, 132
Emotional Authority, 92–100, 130, 131, 132
explorer/discoverer, 151, 152–153, 154–155, 157

G Center, 140, 147
gates
    about, 159–161
    affirmations for, 161–164
    learning about, 170
Generators, 34–46, 131
global solutionist, 151–152, 154, 156

Head Center, 137, 146
heretic, 151–152
hermit, 151
hexagrams, 15
Hindu Brahmin chakra system, 13–14
human design
    basics of, 13–14
    chart for, 16–18
    continuing journey with, 170–171
    experimenting with living, 18
    further exploration of, 169–170
    science behind, 15

I Ching (The Book of Changes), 13, 15
identifying, 10–11
intimate friend, 151, 153, 155
investigator, 151

Kabbalah, 14
knowledge seeker, 151, 152–153, 155, 156

Lunar Authority, 125–129, 133

Manifesting Generators, 47–60, 131–132
Manifestors, 21–33, 130–131
martyr, 151
Mental/Environmental Authority, 121–125, 132

natural genius, 151, 153–154, 156–157
neutrinos, 15

old soul guide, 152, 154–155, 156–157
opportunist, 151

physical senses, 9
Primary Health System (PHS), 171
Profiles
    about, 150
    meanings of, 152–157
    6 Lines of the Hexagram and, 151–152
    understanding, 170
Projectors, 61–75, 132

Ra Uru Hu, 13, 15, 166
readings, 170–171
Reflectors, 76–89, 133
role model, 152
Root Center, 145, 148

Sacral Authority, 101–104, 131–132
Sacral Center, 144, 148
Self-Projected/G Center Authority, 117–120,
    132
Solar Plexus Center, 143, 148
Splenic Authority, 105–108, 131, 132
Splenic Center, 142, 147
strategy and authority (S&A), 130–133, 169

Throat Center, 139, 147
Tree of Life, 14
types
    about, 20
    Generators, 34–46, 131
    Manifesting Generators, 47–60, 131–132
    Manifestors, 21–33, 130–131
    Projectors, 61–75, 132
    Reflectors, 76–89, 133
    understanding, 169

undefined centers, 146–148

Voice, The, 13, 15

Western astrology, 13

Zohar/Kabbalistic tradition, 14

Inspiring | Educating | Creating | Entertaining

Brimming with creative inspiration, how-to projects, and useful information to enrich your everyday life, quarto.com is a favorite destination for those pursuing their interests and passions.

First Published in 2023 by Fair Winds Press, an imprint of The Quarto Group, 100 Cummings Center, Suite 265-D, Beverly, MA 01915, USA.
T (978) 282-9590 F (978) 283-2742 Quarto.com

Fair Winds Press titles are also available at discount for retail, wholesale, promotional, and bulk purchase. For details, contact the Special Sales Manager by email at specialsales@quarto.com or by mail at The Quarto Group, Attn: Special Sales Manager, 100 Cummings Center, Suite 265-D, Beverly, MA 01915, USA.

27 26 25 24 23   1 2 3 4 5

ISBN: 978-0-7603-7914-1
Digital edition published in 2023
eISBN: 978-0-7603-7915-8

Library of Congress Cataloging-in-Publication Data available.

Design: Kelley Galbreath
Cover Image: Shutterstock
Illustration: Maggie Cote 5, 14, 17, 20, 21, 34, 47, 61, 76, 92, 101, 105, 109, 113, 117, 121, 125, 135–145, 160, 167. Ada Grace Keesler 25, 28, 38, 51, 66, 79, 95-97, 168.
Images: Shutterstock 5 (background), 32, 45, 59, 74, 87, 90, 100, 149. Unsplash 8 (Valerie Blanchett), 19 (Marissa Rodriguez), 134 (Valeriia Kogan), 158 (Eberhard Grossgasteiger), 165 (Carolinie Cavalli).

Printed in China

The information in this book is for educational purposes only. It is not intended to replace the advice of a physician or medical practitioner. Please see your health-care provider before beginning any new health program.